MW00479776

The Potential and Power of Prayer

THE

Potential and Power of Prayer

How to Unleash
the Praying Church

Chuck Lawless

THOM S. RAINER, SERIES EDITOR

TYNDALE
MOMENTUM®

A Tyndale nonfiction imprint

Visit Tyndale online at tyndale.com.

Visit Tyndale Momentum online at tyndalemomentum.com.

Tyndale, Tyndale's quill logo, *Tyndale Momentum*, and the Tyndale Momentum logo are registered trademarks of Tyndale House Ministries. Tyndale Momentum is a nonfiction imprint of Tyndale House Publishers, Carol Stream, Illinois.

The Potential and Power of Prayer: How to Unleash the Praying Church

Designed by Ron C. Kaufmann

For information about special discounts for bulk purchases, please contact Tyndale House Publishers at csresponse@tyndale.com, or call 1-855-277-9400.

Library of Congress Cataloging-in-Publication Data

A catalog record for this book is available from the Library of Congress.

ISBN 978-1-4964-6200-8

Printed in the United States of America

28	27	26	25	24	23	22
7	6	5	4	3	2	1

To Pam,
my bride, my friend, my prayer partner.

To Danny Akin,
president of the Southeastern Baptist Theological Seminary,
who has led our seminary to be a praying institution.

To Jeremy,
my administrative assistant and friend,
who prayed for me, protected my time, and served
as editor to make this work possible.

Contents

Why No Power?

I STARTED MY FIRST pastorate when I was twenty years old. As you might imagine, I had no idea what I was doing. That small country church knew me through one of their previous pastors, and I suspect I was the best they could afford at the time. The nineteen people who made up the congregation that first Sunday could hardly pay anything close to a full-time salary, but I was willing to take anything for the opportunity to preach.

I had become a believer at the age of thirteen, and I faithfully attended church. But attendance didn't mean I was strongly or intentionally discipled. I did the best I could to walk with Christ, but with very little equipping for the task. Still, I was certain that God was calling me to preach, and the invitation from that little church in southwestern Ohio lit my fire for ministry.

I wish I could say that the lay leaders in that church were

thoroughly equipped and ready to help their young, rookie pastor do his job, but that was not the case. They were great people who loved the Lord, but no one had intentionally discipled most of them, either. In many respects, I was a baby believer leading other baby believers. And though most of the congregation was older than I was, they didn't know much more than I did about following Jesus.

However, there were three things we knew we had to do: *preach the Bible, tell others about Jesus*, and *pray*. I cringe to think about my sermons in those days; in fact, I'm glad I preached them at a time when cassette tapes were state of the art rather than internet streaming. Still, I was convinced I needed to preach the Word, and I did the best I could. The church members were gracious enough to affirm my preaching even as they prayed for me to improve.

Those same members, despite their own lack of training, loved telling others about Jesus. They told their family members, their coworkers, their neighbors, their classmates, and anyone else who would listen (and, I'm certain, some folks who did *not* want to listen). Every Sunday, they told me stories about evangelizing people in our community, and our church began to grow. Week after week, we had the privilege of baptizing new believers. Within two years, our little church of nineteen saw more than one hundred baptisms of new Christ-followers. I found it especially exciting that many of these new believers were parents, grandparents, children, grandchildren, and cousins of our church members. So productive were our evangelism efforts that we grieved as a congregation if a week passed without someone coming to Christ.

How did we get there? We prayed. A lot. Together and individually. Passionately and persistently. Faithfully and fiercely. We prayed because we didn't know what else to do. And God blessed our efforts.

The Motive behind Our Prayers

Looking back, I realize that we prayed for at least four reasons.

First, we were desperate for God to do something among us and through us. The church had been through tough times for several years prior to my coming as pastor. The congregation of nineteen people had once listed more than a hundred regular attenders, but strife and division had decimated the church. We knew that only God's intervention would enable us to survive and thrive. Desperation is a good thing when it drives us to our knees before our heavenly Father.

Second, we realized we had no idea what we were doing as a church. I certainly did not—and I was the pastor! I had never performed a baptism, led the Lord's Supper, offered premarital or marital counseling, created a church budget, or moderated a business meeting. So I prayed. The few remaining members were wearing many hats, tackling multiple responsibilities, and giving their all to tasks for which they were not always gifted. So they prayed. Just like desperation, recognizing our inability pushes us to pray.

Third, we wanted our loved ones and friends to get saved, but we knew we could never change their hearts on our own. We didn't spend much time thinking theologically about their separation from God, yet we knew from experience the hardened hearts of some of the people we loved. We knew them well enough to know that God would have to intervene if they were ever to respond to the gospel. In some cases, we knew how many times in the past they had refused to even listen. So we prayed. And we kept praying until God answered. Like desperation and inability, a deep burden for nonbelievers compels us to pray.

Fourth, prayer was something that every member of our church family could do. Men prayed together. Women prayed together. Men and women prayed together. Young believers who knew nothing about prayer talked to God the best they knew how. In fact, their passion for God sometimes exceeded that of others in the church who had been believers far longer. Teenagers prayed, sometimes challenging their parents with their heartbrokenness for nonbelieving classmates and friends. Even the young kids prayed at times—and there is nothing like hearing a preschooler or a grade schooler talk to God with childlike openness and honesty. In our congregation, kneeling in prayer (literally and figuratively) put us all on the same level, regardless of our status in the community or in the church. Praying together made us even more like a family.

I am a strong believer in teaching people how to pray more effectively, but I am thankful that no one requires significant training to simply talk to God. The youngest, least-trained believer can pray, and the smallest, least-trained church can see God work when they pray faithfully and persistently. When prayer becomes part of the DNA of a church, God's power is released.

You will hear me speak often about getting prayer into the DNA of our churches. By DNA, I mean a fundamental commitment or foundation that characterizes the church. When something—such as prayer—is so ingrained in a church that they (and others) equate the church with that commitment, that's DNA-level stuff. I want people to know your church as a congregation that takes prayer seriously, continually turns to God for guidance, and sees answers to their prayers. For now, ask yourself these probing (perhaps even uncomfortable) questions:

"Is prayer in *my* DNA?"

"Is prayer in the DNA of my church?"

The Struggle of Prayer

In my mind's eye, I can still see those folks from my first church, even though my ministry with them was several decades ago. Since then, I have pastored another church in Ohio for more than eleven years, taught at a seminary for more than twenty-five years, worked with a mission agency, served as an interim pastor in several churches, and studied church growth in North America and around the world. Through all those roles and responsibilities, I've learned that my experience with prayer in that little church is more the exception than the rule. In fact, I have drawn several conclusions that led to the writing of this book.

- Becoming a praying church is not as easy as it sounds.

- As churches seek to grow, they often focus more on demographics and internal issues than on spiritual matters.

- Many believers have never learned to pray because no one intentionally taught them to pray.

- Many who once leaned on God in prayerful dependence now too often lean on themselves.

- A lack of prayer goes hand in hand with a lack of knowledge of the Word of God.

- Prayer ministries usually start small, grow slowly, and seldom involve every church member.

Let's look at each of these in turn.

Becoming a praying church is not as easy as it sounds.

In my first church in Ohio, we did not know how to pray well, but we did make our requests known to God with great abandon.

We simply did what the apostle Paul commanded: "Don't worry about anything; instead, pray about everything. Tell God what you need, and thank him for all he has done" (Philippians 4:6). When I moved to my second pastorate, I went to a larger church with more staff and more activities, and I learned that ministry can sometimes get in the way of prayer. Even those of us who know better can preach and teach about prayer without really praying. We talk about it more than we do it.

In my years as a church consultant, I've been surprised by the number of churches seeking outside assistance who have not made it a priority to *pray* about their needs. I often ask these churches whether they have a prayer team who will support us as we work together. Rarely is there a team already in place. Some churches have a prayer ministry leader (and it is seldom the pastor, which we'll discuss later), but they have not made the connection between their recognized need for outside consulting and their more important need for God's power. Their praying as a church has been largely limited to praying for the physical needs of the congregation. That is *not* DNA-level prayer.

One problem, I suspect, is that congregations often lose the passion for prayer that drove my first church to their knees. As a church sees steady growth, develops programming and structure, and hires staff to do the work, their desperation for God wanes. In turn, a lack of desperation undermines the second thing that pushes us to pray: recognizing our inabilities. When we start to believe we can do ministry on our own, we think we don't need to pray as much.

Next, losing a sense of burden for the lost decreases our urgency to pray. I suspect that many members of evangelical churches today are not entirely convinced that a personal relationship with Christ is necessary for salvation—even though Jesus says in John 14:6 that he is the only way to God. In fact, a 2020 study showed that 48 percent of adults in America believe that "if a person is generally good, or does enough good things during their life, they will 'earn' a place in Heaven."[1] The same study showed that 41 percent of evangelicals believe in a works-based salvation by "being or doing good."[2] If good people can go to heaven apart from an encounter with Jesus, evangelism is hardly necessary. If evangelism isn't necessary, why worry about praying for those who claim no relationship with Jesus? Seemingly capable, self-dependent congregations with little or no burden for nonbelievers simply do not pray well.

To be honest, even those of us who long to depend on God, who recognize our inabilities and carry a burden for the lost, still sometimes struggle to pray consistently. Our theology may push us toward prayer, but our practice lags behind. Several causes (noted below) contribute to this failure, but the conclusion is the same: Praying as a church is seldom as easy as it seemed in my first days of ministry.

As churches seek to grow, they often focus more on demographics and internal issues than on spiritual matters.

In church growth circles, we often refer to three sets of factors that affect a church's growth: *contextual factors*, *institutional factors*, and *spiritual factors*.[3] Contextual factors are outside issues—political, sociological, cultural, and environmental—over which the church has no control.[4] For example, changes in population or demographics may contribute to a church's growth or decline. Globally, persecution is another contextual factor, though history teaches that persecution of the church often leads to growth rather than decline.

Institutional factors are internal issues over which the church has some control. These might include such things as church polity, leadership direction, financial commitments, and unresolved conflicts. Institutional factors in nongrowing churches are often wrapped up in unhealthy traditionalism.

Spiritual factors, on the other hand, are factors "in the heavenlies"—that is, governed by the sovereign work of the Holy Spirit, who is "not subject to contextual or institutional factors."[5] An emphasis on prayer (or lack thereof) may be an institutional factor, but the *power* of prayer is a spiritual one. Apart from prayer, we can tackle issues in the church only on an earthly level.

Churches who are focused on growth tend to address contextual factors (such as demographics) and institutional factors (such as programming), but they give little attention to the spiritual factors of individual and corporate prayer. If they do address prayer, it is often because they know they *should* rather than because they see it as a lifeline for the congregation. Part of my purpose in writing is to address the need to do something different.

Many believers have never learned to pray because no one intentionally taught them to pray.

Many churches are guilty of *telling* believers to pray without *teaching* them how to do it. The result is frustration—Christians who want to be obedient to God in prayer but are not certain how to do it. Even many courses on prayer are more focused on the transfer of information than the practice of prayer. And then pastors and other church leaders become frustrated with their members for not doing what they haven't taught them to do!

Most churches *talk* about prayer. Churches with prayer in their DNA actually *pray*. Which of these comparisons best illustrates your church?

- Churches that *talk* about prayer schedule prayer meetings (which relatively few members attend). Churches with prayer in their DNA *pray* at their prayer meetings.

- Churches that *talk* about prayer may *preach* about prayer. Churches with prayer in their DNA *preach* about prayer and *pray* about preaching.

- Churches that *talk* about prayer may have a prayer list. Churches with prayer in their DNA consistently and intentionally *pray through* their prayer list and report God's answers.

- Churches that *talk* about prayer may have a prayer ministry—among others. Churches with prayer in their DNA have a prayer ministry that *covers in prayer* every other ministry.

- Churches that *talk* about prayer have leaders who *talk* about prayer. Churches with prayer in their DNA have leaders who *model* prayer.

- Churches that *talk* about prayer respond *reactively* to the enemy's attacks. Churches with prayer in their DNA *pray proactively* in preparation for the enemy's attacks.

- Churches that *talk* about prayer *hope* God will do great things. Churches with prayer in their DNA *expect* God to do great things.

- Churches that *talk* about prayer do *not* threaten the enemy. Churches with prayer in their DNA *make the devil shake*.[6]

Because our churches have not done a good job of teaching people how to pray, many Christians have learned only by observing others. Unfortunately, one thing they've learned is to pray *reactively* rather than *proactively*.[7]

Think about prayer in your church. If you have a prayer list, what does it usually take to get your name on it? In many cases, it takes a sickness or tragedy. When we learn about the problem, we pray. Likewise, we pray for families when they are struggling; for young people who are wandering; and for other churches when we hear they are fighting or when their pastor leaves. Responding to needs in prayer isn't *wrong*, but how much stronger would our churches and our families be if we consistently prayed for one another *before* trouble sets in?

Seminary students I have taught over the years most often tell me that prayer is the most difficult spiritual discipline to maintain. They know they should be praying, but that knowledge doesn't always translate into disciplined action. When I ask these future church leaders about their role models—about the people who taught them how to pray—few are able to name *anyone*. They have learned to pray on their own, if they've learned at all.

I fear that the leaders in our churches, our Christian universities, and our seminaries are not only struggling with prayer themselves, but are also sending out the next generations of believers who share the same struggle. I'm concerned that we are producing prayerless pastors who are shepherding prayerless and powerless churches. One consequence is that we are sending missionaries to the front lines with only superficial prayer support.

Many who once leaned on God in prayerful dependence now too often lean on themselves.

As an educator, I believe wholeheartedly in training, but I fear we may educate our students out of dependence on God. Even the best church leaders who ran to God in prayer when they first entered ministry now sometimes rely on their education, their experience, and their track record more than they rely on God. That kind of prayerlessness—to which we all are susceptible—is simply "idolatry of the self."[8]

Prayerful dependence on God—both for churches and individuals—is not our default setting. Individually and corporately, we may start out leaning on God, but then retreat into self-dependence and only perfunctory prayer. We may mask our prayerlessness with busyness for God, but unless we halt it early, spiritual decline sets in.

Far too easily, we become like the disciples of Jesus in Mark 9:14-29, who tried to heal a demon-possessed boy. The boy's father had brought him to the disciples, surely because he had heard they had the power to exorcise demons. Jesus had previously sent out the twelve disciples on a ministry tour, and "they cast out many demons and healed many sick people, anointing them with olive oil" (Mark 6:13). On another occasion, he sent out seventy-two other disciples, who were so successful that, when they reported back to Jesus, they said, "Lord, even the demons obey us when we use your name!" (Luke 10:17).

However, that was not the case this time. The grieving father's words to Jesus were simple, clear, and tragic: "I asked your disciples to cast out the evil spirit, *but they couldn't do it*" (Mark 9:18, italics added). Despite their previous success, something was different this time. Whatever it was, it left the boy in agony and the father struggling with his faith. His plaintive words to Jesus, "I do believe, but help me overcome my unbelief!" (Mark 9:24) revealed not only his internal conflict, but also the disciples' failure to strengthen this man's faith when they had the opportunity.

Later, when the disciples asked Jesus privately about their failure, he told them, "This kind can be cast out only by prayer"

(Mark 9:29). Apparently, they had tried to cast out the demon without praying.

Matthew 17:20 tells us they also lacked faith—"even as small as a mustard seed"—so they had entered this encounter without much going for them. Whatever the reason, they didn't pray, which meant they tried to cast out a demon in their own power. Perhaps because of their previous success, they relied solely on their own ability in this case to try to do life-changing ministry. But they failed miserably and would have left the boy in bondage had Jesus not intervened.

I'm afraid this is the way, too often, we do ministry and lead our churches. Early in our Christian walk, we relied on God and his power. But sometimes, over time, the tensions and struggles of Christian living and ministry weaken our faith. At other times, we unintentionally rely on our own strength to do God's work; after all, if we were successful yesterday, we will surely be successful today. Prayer loses its place in our lives, and we fight today's battles based on "yesterday's power."[9]

Eventually, we fall into the trap of prayerlessness, which the late Jack Taylor defined years ago as "that state in which one prays less than he ought, less than the Father desires, and less than [he] himself knows he should."[10] Even though we know better, we still do not pray like we should. And as John Onwuchekwa writes in his 2018 book on prayer, "Prayerlessness is spiritual suicide."[11]

A lack of prayer goes hand in hand with a lack of knowledge of the Word of God.

A 2019 Lifeway Research study found that 32 percent of those who attend church at least once a month read the Bible daily, and a majority of churchgoers (59 percent) read the Bible at least a few times a week.[12] In my years as a pastor, however, I observed that merely reading the Bible doesn't necessarily lead to increased, retained knowledge of the Scriptures. For some people, Bible reading is a "check the box" discipline that includes little meditation or memorization of the Word.

But when we dig into God's Word regularly, it is difficult not to see *prayer* throughout the Bible. Some years ago, I looked for every reference to prayer as I read through the Bible in a year, and I highlighted each one with a blue highlighter. I saw prayer mentioned so often that I finished my reading most days with a deepened burden to pray more. Sometimes I immediately set my Bible aside, buried my face in the floor, and prayed because of what I had read.

I wish I could list all the references here, but maybe this sample from a portion of the Old Testament will whet your appetite to search the Scriptures for more. (We will cover examples from the New Testament in later chapters.)

- Abraham intercedes for the righteous in Sodom (Genesis 18:16–19:16)

- Moses prays for the people who created the golden calf (Exodus 32:11-14)

- Moses prays for the complaining people (Numbers 11:1-3)

- Joshua prays when his warriors lose the battle at Ai (Joshua 7:6-9)

- Gideon asks for signs from the Lord (Judges 6)

- Hannah prays to have a child (1 Samuel 1:9-16)

- David seeks direction about attacking the Philistines (2 Samuel 5:19)

- Solomon prays at the dedication of the Temple
  (1 Kings 8:22-53)

- Hezekiah prays for a longer life (2 Kings 20:1-11)

- Jehoshaphat prays in a time of war (2 Chronicles 20:3-13)

- Nehemiah prays as he mourns the distress of the people
  in Jerusalem (Nehemiah 1:4-11)

- David prays about deliverance from his enemies
  (Psalm 3:1-7); about thirsting for God (Psalm 63);
  about God's knowledge of us (Psalm 139); and about
  our need for God's help (Psalm 142:1-7)

- David prays for forgiveness for his sin with Bathsheba
  (Psalm 51)

- Jeremiah prays about purchasing a field
  (Jeremiah 32:16-25)

- Daniel prays on behalf of a rebellious people
  (Daniel 9:4-19)

- Jonah prays from the belly of a fish (Jonah 2:1-9)

I could list many other examples of prayer in the Old Testament, but for now, simply allow this truth to sink in: The God of the Bible is a communicating God who invites us to come to him in prayer. He hears the cries of his people, even though sometimes we do not recognize that truth. When we study the stories about prayer in the Bible, we learn a valuable lesson about God's power and faithfulness.

Prayer ministries usually start small, grow slowly, and seldom involve every church member.

As one who has a PhD in evangelism and church growth, I naturally think of *numbers* as one way to evaluate the growth and health of a church. Though I reject an idolatrous fixation with numbers, I agree with a hero of mine from the past, Charles Spurgeon:

> I am not among those who decry statistics, nor do I
> consider that they are productive of all manner of evil;
> for they do much good if they are accurate, and if men
> use them lawfully. It is a good thing for people to see the
> nakedness of the land through statistics of decrease, that
> they may be driven on their knees before the Lord to seek
> prosperity; and, on the other hand, it is by no means an
> evil thing for workers to be encouraged by having some
> account of results set before them. I should be very sorry
> if the practice of adding up, and deducting, and giving in
> the net result were to be abandoned, for it must be right
> to know our numerical condition.[13]

With regard to prayer ministries specifically, I am less concerned about growing large numbers of participants. I certainly want all members praying, but I realize that raising up God-dependent prayer warriors takes time. We must be willing to persevere and run the race well to become a praying church. We must keep running when the work gets hard, and press on toward the finish line together as a congregation.

Prayer ministry is also typically behind the scenes, with little recognition or praise for those who pray. If I determine that I must have a large group to have an effective prayer ministry, it is likely I will not get there easily. On the other hand, a few people who can touch heaven in prayer are better than dozens of participants who are not truly committed to prayer.

If the Lord gives you only a handful of prayer warriors to launch your group, rejoice! Thank him for what he has provided, rather than becoming discouraged because more people are not participating. Start with the faithful few, if necessary, and let the prayer ministry grow at its own pace. Embers of prayer may eventually produce a flame in your church, but you must be patient and persistent.

Hope Forged on Our Knees

I realize the previous section may sound pessimistic. It's hard to read about churches that only talk about prayer but don't teach it, and believers who do not know what the Bible says about prayer or who live in self-dependence, without becoming discouraged. Believe me, that is not my goal. I want to deal honestly with the challenges, but I also see glimmers of hope that make me excited about the potential to create churches with prayer in their DNA.

For example, the seminary where I teach made a commitment several years ago to not only be a great commission seminary, but also a praying one. That's how we responded when two prayer-warrior leaders in our denomination challenged us to make sure we were graduating men and women who know how to pray. Our commitment to address this issue led us to restructure our executive leadership team to free me up to oversee these efforts. Today, we have student-led prayer meetings, faculty prayer gatherings, chapel prayer moments, online prayer meetings, a National Day of Prayer emphasis, weekly classroom prayer requests, and prayer training in our curricular and cocurricular activities. We are just one institution, but I pray others will join us in this effort.

I have also seen a growing attention to prayer in increasing numbers of mentoring relationships among older and younger believers alike. I know many young leaders who want mature Christian mentors, and they are seeking older leaders to show them how to walk well with God. Particularly, they want to address the weaknesses in their lives—which often includes prayer. Having felt the lack of adequate role models, as they admit their need, seek guidance, and strive to grow in grace, they gravitate toward older believers who know God. As long as we can help them connect with prayer-warrior mentors, I have nothing but hope for this young generation as they learn to pray.

I am privileged to have a pastoral mentor, Tom Elliff, who is the most prayerful man I know. I have learned from him by listening to his prayers and reading his books on prayer.[14] I am in my sixties, he is in his upper seventies, and he himself has mentors who are in their nineties! He still learns from them, and I get to learn from him.

When I think about young leaders, my concern is the difficulty of finding prayer mentors like Tom who have time to invest in them. I long to know church leaders who pray in such a way that others come to them to learn their discipline of prayer. My hope is that this book will help produce more prayerful leaders to serve as strong role models—and perhaps you will be one of them.

Through technology and other means, accessibility to believers around the world has made it possible for us to learn how to pray from other brothers and sisters in Christ. Some live in risky places, where desperation, inability, and burden are part of daily life, and prayer is a matter of spiritual survival. Prayer is in their spiritual DNA in ways I seldom see among evangelicals in North America. Three stories come to mind that illustrate this point.

First, a group of believers in Eastern Europe invited me some years ago to lead a prayer training conference in their country.[15] I spent many hours preparing for the training, and I felt equipped and ready to go when the conference began. As we began the meeting, the national leader called us to prayer. Everyone then stood (which was customary, I learned) and began praying aloud one by one. I understood their prayers only through a translator whispering in my ear, but I didn't need to know their language to recognize their passion. They took the privilege of speaking to God on behalf of themselves and others quite seriously. Two hours later—*two hours!*—the leader finally said "amen." Then he invited me up to teach everyone how to pray. What would *you* have said? I may have been the professor in the room, but those Eastern European Christians were *my* teachers.

Second, on the wall in my office across from my desk, I have mounted two prayer mats from a church I visited in East Asia years ago. During their worship service, I watched the believers place their mats on the floor, kneel down, and pray to God as if they were the only person in the room. I had heard about their focus on prayer before I arrived, but experiencing it was something else entirely. I don't have the words to describe the sense of unity and power I felt in that room that day. Now, whenever I see the worn, dirty spots on those two prayer mats on my wall, they remind me of a people who were seeking God with all their heart, soul, and strength. And I want to pray like they prayed.

Third, during the lockdown days of COVID-19 in 2020, our seminary sponsored online prayer meetings, where I was able to meet prayer-focused international believers. Some were feeling isolated and alone, and they welcomed any opportunity to join with other believers in prayer. I am grateful that digital technology offers us all the gift of connection with missionaries and internationals around the world. I encourage you to think of ways that your church might connect with believers overseas simply to pray with them.

A student from Central Asia who participated in one of our prayer meetings stayed awake until the middle of the night to join us live, and I'm glad he did. Prayer matters so much to this young man that he prioritized prayer over sleep. His presence among our students was both refreshing and convicting. In addition to verbalizing prayers on behalf of others, he encouraged us with his faith and challenged us with his trust in God in a most difficult situation. Not many would have made the commitment this brother did to join us for prayer, but I know several people from around the world who would.

Where We're Headed

Before we continue, I want to share with you my presuppositions and my plan for the remaining chapters.

First, I stand on the Word of God. "All Scripture is God-breathed and is useful for teaching, rebuking, correcting and training in righteousness" (2 Timothy 3:16, NIV). By the time you finish this book, I want you to have made a stronger commitment to prayer *and* have a deeper desire to read the Bible. One without the other is insufficient for Christian growth. I make no apologies that the rest of the chapters are filled with Scripture.

Second, every believer and church I know—beginning with myself and my congregation—has room for improvement in prayer. Even the most persistent prayer warriors long to pray more; the more they know God through prayer, the more they want to pray. Likewise, the most prayer-centered churches know they still have room for growth.

Third, everyone can grow in their prayer life, even if that growth is slow or sporadic. Prayer should be a natural and central part of the Christian life. Most of the time, though, we have to *practice it as a habit* before it becomes part of who we are.

If you were to evaluate your prayer life on a scale from one to ten, I assume you would like to move up to a ten as quickly as possible. But it seldom happens that way. Moving up the scale *at all* is a step in the right direction. If you move from even a one to a two as a result of reading this book, I will be pleased. The goal is *progress*, not perfection.

Fourth, this book will address your personal prayer life, but I am most concerned about getting believers to pray *together*. I want to see prayer become embedded in the DNA of churches everywhere. My emphasis on praying with other believers is quite intentional. No one learns how to pray well on their own, and there is tremendous power in corporate prayer as believers agree together and seek God together.

Ultimately, it isn't as important *how* prayer happens or *where* it happens. What matters most is that it *happens*. And the first step in making it happen is for individual believers to commit themselves to prayer. To that end, my approach in this book is *personal*—not because I'm such a great prayer warrior, but precisely because I'm not. I am a fellow traveler with you on this journey, and I still have a lot to learn.

Finally, let me lay out the plan for the rest of the book so you'll know where we're going.

In chapter 2, we'll talk about what prayer is and why it matters. I will give you my definition of prayer and introduce you to a description of prayer that really speaks to my heart. My hope is that you'll finish the chapter with a greater desire to pray.

Chapter 3 will take us into the Bible in a concentrated way. We will examine Jesus' prayer in the Gospel of Luke and the early church's prayer in the book of Acts. These two books are not the only ones in the Bible that address these topics, but they provide a good example of history-changing prayer. Studying the prayer lives of Jesus and the early church should produce a strong conviction and a heartfelt desire to pray more.

Chapter 4 focuses on the relationship between prayer and spiritual warfare. Paul warned us in no uncertain terms that we are fighting against supernatural principalities and powers (Ephesians 6:12). He didn't want us to miss the reality of the battle, but neither did he want us to fear it. This chapter focuses particularly on praying for the work of evangelism.

Chapter 5 addresses leaders in general, but focuses specifically on pastors, who are typically the primary role models in a praying church. As I wrote this chapter, I thought of ways I might have prayed better when I was a full-time pastor. The churches I led probably would have prayed more if I had led the way more intentionally.

Frankly, I am grateful for any opportunity I have today to help churches pray, because I look back with some regret. If you are a pastor, I hope chapter 5 challenges you to pray more. But even if you're not a pastor, I hope this chapter will inspire you to pray more for your pastor and other church leaders. Everyone will be stronger when we intercede for one another.

Chapter 6 broadens the focus to include the entire congregation. Praying together matters, but many churches lose their intentional focus on prayer. They must then choose to restart their prayer effort. How they do that will vary by congregation. This chapter offers several practical ideas for churches who want prayer to become part of their DNA.

A brief final chapter concludes with a caution to prayer warriors and a challenge to church leaders. These closing thoughts may surprise you in a book about prayer, but I trust they will make sense to you by the time you arrive there.

Conclusion

As we conclude this chapter, this is my prayer for you:

> *Father, I praise you for who you are: a personal God who communicates with us and invites us to your throne in prayer. I thank you for praying role models—even if we have only a few of them—who push us and equip us to pray more. I pray that some who read this book will be role models in prayer for multiple generations.*
>
> *I thank you, God, for my readers. Wherever they may serve in your Kingdom's work, teach them to pray so that they might teach others. May they find so much peace and power on their knees that they continually want to meet you there. Father, let it be for all of us!*
>
> *In Jesus' name, amen.*

2

What Prayer Is, and Why It Matters

As a pastor, I do my best to talk with the young kids in my church—to listen to them and hear what they're thinking. I love kneeling to their level after a church service and simply giving them attention as Pastor Chuck. I want them to get to know me when they are young so they will feel comfortable hearing me and trusting me as they grow. Even now, on my refrigerator, I have a picture that one of the little girls in our congregation drew for me.

Kids can be really honest . . . and funny. I recently reviewed some children's books and watched a few videos about kids and their understanding of prayer. Defining prayer isn't easy, and I wanted to hear from some people who communicate well at a child's level.

Here's what I learned from the kids: Prayer is "talking to God," "asking him for stuff," and "saying thank you" to him. Sometimes we pray to tell God we're sad, and sometimes to tell him we're sorry. But prayer always means talking to God. In the children's book *God Gave Us Prayer*, Mama fox encourages Little Pup to pray: "Just keep talking to him, sweet one, all the time. That's why God gave us prayer. So we could talk to him any part of the day."

"Or night!" Little Pup chimes in.[1]

Our posture in prayer also matters—at least according to kids. People who pray should close their eyes, bow their heads, fold their arms, and maybe kneel down. They shouldn't peek or look around—nor should they fall asleep. And it's probably best to pray short prayers, especially when you are waiting to eat!

I happen to agree with the recommendation for short prayers, but the purpose of this chapter is more than simply offering some prayer guidelines. My aim is to define prayer and establish its significance. I want you to see that prayer truly matters in all we do as believers. And I want people to pray more, both individually and congregationally.

Personal Reflection: How do you define *prayer*? Take a minute and write your own definition.

What Prayer Is

Many speakers and writers have offered their definitions of prayer, and those definitions vary only slightly. Which of the examples below comes closest to your own definition of prayer?

- Prayer "is established (perhaps even defined as) calling on God to come through on his promises."[2]

- "We can define prayer as a *personal, communicative response to the knowledge of God.*"[3]

- "Prayer is discourse with the personal God Himself."[4]

- "Prayer is communion with God in order to . . .

  1. Intimately know, love, and worship Him. . . .
  2. Understand and conform our lives to His will and ways. . . .
  3. Access and advance His kingdom, power, and glory."[5]

- Prayer is "the act of communicating with God as an expression of trust in him."[6]

These authors are all much wiser than I am, but my own definition is similar: *Prayer is communicating with God.*[7] Often, I will add a clarifying description: Prayer is an *expression* of our *relationship* with God and a *confession* of our *dependence* on him.

To help us grasp what prayer means, let me unpack both statements, beginning with the definition. I realize my definition is simple and brief, but behind the words are several important concepts.

Prayer is communicating with God.

That fact that we can communicate with almighty God ought to amaze us, overwhelm us, and drive us to our knees—all at the same time. I especially feel that way after I have visited places and people in the world who worship gods they have made with their own hands. Often seen sitting on a shelf in the corner of the room, these gods have eyes but they cannot see, mouths but they cannot speak, and ears but they cannot hear. They have no life in them at all. Nevertheless, I have watched as their followers bow before them and pray to them with religious zeal—and I grieve for them because I know their god isn't listening. I also know the joy of having a relationship with the true and living God who does listen.

Our God is hardly a figurine on a shelf. He is everywhere. He is all-powerful. He knows all things past, present, and future. The God of the Bible spoke creation into existence. He conversed with Adam and Eve, the first human beings. He pursued them when they rejected his commands, provided coverings for them after they had sinned, and put into action a plan to save them from their sin. This God called out a people through Abraham, and he communicated with his people through prophets, priests, and kings.

At just the right time, God himself came to earth in the person of Jesus Christ, the baby born in Bethlehem. Whereas previously God had spoken through the prophets, "now in these final days, he has spoken to us through his Son" (Hebrews 1:2). Jesus lived a sinless life and then died on the cross for us; he was our substitute who bore the penalty for our sin. Death could not hold him, however, and he conquered death through resurrection. In his time, he will return again as King of kings and Lord of lords. In the words of J. I. Packer, this God is *personal, plural* [trinitarian], *perfect, powerful, purposeful, a promise keeper, paternal,* and *praiseworthy.*"[8]

This is our God—and you and I are privileged to pray to him. Stephen Kendrick and Alex Kendrick put it this way: "If we could only understand what being in the presence of the Almighty is truly like, our mind wouldn't be casually wandering. We wouldn't be drifting in and out of sleep. We'd be fully alert and overwhelmed. All attention held captive. Stunned. Speechless."[9]

When we remember that we are talking to *God,* our prayers won't be flippant. We will pray as he commands, for he is Almighty. We will pray according to his will because we know his way is always right. We will pray with humility, knowing that only his grace allows us to approach him. When we ask for anything in prayer, we want to know he is pleased with that request. And because we know he makes no mistakes, we won't get frustrated with him when his answer is "wait" or "no."

• • •

Before we go further in this chapter, I want to challenge you to respond briefly to what you have read. Pause now and thank God that you have the opportunity to speak to him. Communicate with him right now—and know that he hears you. Be amazed by that fact!

• • •

At its foundation, prayer assumes we have a relationship with God. We are able to speak to God not because we are worthy on our own merits, but because he has welcomed us into a relationship with himself through Jesus Christ. That relationship is the basis for our communication with God. He graciously invites us into his presence and receives us there.

In return, he wants us to *seek* him. He wants us to *want* to come to him. He desires for us to deliberately and humbly set our hearts and minds on him:

> If my people who are called by my name will humble
> themselves and pray and seek my face and turn from their
> wicked ways, I will hear from heaven and will forgive
> their sins and restore their land.
>
> 2 CHRONICLES 7:14

> Search for the LORD and for his strength; continually
> seek him.
>
> PSALM 105:4

> The LORD is close to all who call on him, yes, to all who
> call on him in truth.
>
> PSALM 145:18

Seek the LORD while you can find him. Call on him now while he is near.

ISAIAH 55:6

If you look for me wholeheartedly, you will find me.

JEREMIAH 29:13

Come to me, all of you who are weary and carry heavy burdens, and I will give you rest.

MATTHEW 11:28

Let us come boldly to the throne of our gracious God. There we will receive his mercy, and we will find grace to help us when we need it most.

HEBREWS 4:16

Come close to God, and God will come close to you.

JAMES 4:8

Isn't it amazing? The God who made all things wants us to have a relationship with him. He wants us to come to him and depend on him. And he wants us to communicate with him through prayer. In fact, he welcomes us as his children.

My wife and I do not have children, but we have longstanding relationships with former church members and with students we claim as our kids. In some cases, they send us cards on Mother's Day and Father's Day. Their own children know us as Mamaw and Papaw. Most of these friends live far from us, but we stay in touch through email, texts, and phone calls.

I prefer phone calls, hands down, because I love to hear their voices. My eyes light up when I see their familiar names on my caller ID. I *want* them to want to talk to me. I want to know their joys and their heartaches. I want them to feel safe coming to me with their struggles. Even a few minutes with one of my "kids" can make any day a good day. If I as a fatherly friend delight when I hear their voices, how much more does our heavenly Father delight when we run to him as his children?

In my definition of prayer, I use the word *communicating* for two reasons. First, communicating with God is essential to our relationship with him. Second, communicating is a two-way interaction. I cannot overemphasize the importance of listening to God through his Word, even as we speak to him in prayer. I fear too many believers are willing to tell God what they need, but they don't listen for his response—which often comes through the Scriptures. When we speak but don't listen, our communication is one-sided.

When we pay little attention to the Scriptures, we may miss teachings directly connected to our praying. For example, the prophet Isaiah spoke these words to the Israelites, who were in rebellion at the time: "Listen! The LORD's arm is not too weak to save you, nor is his ear too deaf to hear you call. It's your sins that have cut you off from God. Because of your sins, he has turned away and will not listen anymore" (Isaiah 59:1-2). God was not willing to hear their prayers if they ignored what he had commanded them. He could *hear*, but he would not *listen* while their rebellion stood in the way.

The writer of Psalm 66, on the other hand, knew what it means to pray when our sins are forgiven:

If I had not confessed the sin in my heart, the Lord would not have listened. But God did listen! He paid attention

to my prayer. Praise God, who did not ignore my prayer
or withdraw his unfailing love from me.

PSALM 66:18-20

Because the psalmist did not deny his sin, but instead confessed
it and turned from it, his relationship with God was good and God
listened to his prayer. The psalmist listened to God and heeded his
Word, and God listened to him as well.

Jesus also connected the Word and prayer: "If you remain in
me and my words remain in you, you may ask for anything you
want, and it will be granted!" (John 15:7). To *remain* in Jesus
means to follow him in daily obedience, forsaking sin and trusting
him as he leads. Remaining in Jesus, though, cannot be separated
from knowing and obeying his teaching; thus, being saturated
with God's Word is a necessity. When we know Jesus, we seek
to know his Word, and we also turn to his Word to know how
best to follow him. Christians who live this way will see their
prayers answered because their requests will reflect the heart and
will of God.

Here is how Ben Patterson, campus pastor at Westmont
College in California, describes the relationship between the Bible
and prayer—or, in the context of this chapter, between listening to
God through his Word and speaking to God in prayer:

> Prayer, like language, begins with being able to hear. Prayer
> starts not when we speak to God but when God speaks to
> us. In the beginning was the Word; God's word, not ours.
> Before all time, before you and I were, was the Word; the
> Light that gives light and life to everyone. There would
> be no speech if God had not first spoken. We would have
> nothing to say if God had not first said something to

us. Ultimately then, all our prayers are answers to God's prayer—his gracious Word of love to us![10]

Andrew Murray, a nineteenth-century South African pastor who wrote extensively about prayer, said this: "Prayer is not monologue, but dialogue; God's voice in response to mine in its most essential part."[11] Hence, I use the word *communicating* in my definition of prayer to remind us of the nonnegotiable connection between listening and speaking.

Prayer is an expression of our relationship with God.

I grew up in a home and local culture where relationships were valued, but were not emphasized like they are in much of the world. Getting things done was more important than getting to know someone. In some ways because of that upbringing, I can be quite impatient in relationships with people who value connection above productivity.

But as I have traveled around the world and worked with people from other cultures, I have learned a lot about the importance of relationships. When working cross-culturally, we show respect for the other person by following a culturally acceptable mode of greeting, and we show that we value other people by spending time with them. Taking two or three hours to have some tea and a conversation while playing checkers is the expected norm in some places. We honor the other person by prioritizing *talk* and *time*.

On a more personal level, I think of my relationship with my wife, Pam. She and I met when two matchmaking church secretaries decided it would be good to introduce us. We met at a single-adults Christmas party, and we began dating about a year later. During that first year, we talked at various other events, and we have now been talking and spending time together for more than thirty years. When I travel, I talk with her on the way to the airport, when I get to the airport, as I am boarding the plane, when I disembark, when I get in my rental car, and when I arrive at my place of ministry. I love to hear her voice, and I trust she likes to hear mine.

I see prayer in a similar way. I love to hear God's voice, and I trust he likes to hear mine. Prayer assumes that we *want* to talk to God as his children; that we are willing to *take the time* to do it; and that we actually *do* spend focused time talking to him.

At its core, prayer is an exclamation, a strong indication of our relationship with God. It may only be silent prayer in the middle of our day somewhere, but it reaches from our hearts to the heart of God the Father. It announces, "I am your child, God, and our relationship is so genuine and deep that we make time to talk together."

Prayer is a confession of our dependence on God.

When we pray, we express our need for God. Think about the model prayer that Jesus teaches his disciples in Matthew 6:9-13 and Luke 11:2-4. Apart from God, we can do *nothing*. We need him to accomplish his will in our lives and on earth. We need him to provide our daily bread, jobs, health, shelter, clothing, transportation, finances, guidance, grace, and rest.[12] The list is endless. We need him to forgive us, and we need him to help us forgive others. We need him to guard us from temptation and deliver us from the evil one.

In short, we need him for *everything*, and prayer is how we express that need. In the words of J. I. Packer, "Before God's throne we *are* all beggars, and begging good gifts from God is what petitionary prayer is all about. We ask God, as beggars, for what we need because he invites us to do so."[13] God wants to meet our needs, but he also wants us to *acknowledge* our need and *ask* him to meet our needs, out of our relationship with him. Thus, prayer says both, "God, I *love* you" and "God, I *need* you."

The opposite is also true, by the way. When we *don't* pray, we are saying to God, in effect, "I don't really love you like I say I do" and "I don't need you very much." For a professing believer, prayerlessness is blatant hypocrisy. It is arrogant denial for those who claim to love God and say they need him. As D. A. Carson notes, prayerlessness "is out of step with the Bible, which portrays what Christian living should be."[14] That conclusion ought to at least catch our attention if we are not praying.

So, what is prayer? It is communicating with God and expressing our love and our need for him. It is both gift and obligation, privilege and responsibility, discipline and delight. It characterizes those who know him, for true believers will pray.

Why Prayer Matters

In some ways, this chapter has already explained why prayer matters. We pray because we love God, and he invites us to come to him. From first mention—"At that time people began to call on the name of the LORD" (Genesis 4:26, NIV)—to today, prayer has been our God-given means to communicate with him. That alone is enough reason to pray. The following reasons also remind us why prayer matters.

We pray because God commands us to pray.

God invites us to pray and expects us to pray. In fact, he even commands us to pray. Jesus assumed his followers would pray. In the Sermon on the Mount, he repeatedly says "when you pray . . . when you pray . . . when you pray" (Matthew 6:5-9; see also Mark 11:25). He also told the parable of the persistent widow to show his disciples "that they should always pray and never give up" (Luke 18:1).

The apostle Paul also challenged the church to pray:

Pray in the Spirit at all times and on every occasion. Stay alert and be persistent in your prayers for all believers everywhere.
EPHESIANS 6:18

Don't worry about anything; instead, pray about everything. Tell God what you need, and thank him for all he has done.
PHILIPPIANS 4:6

Devote yourselves to prayer with an alert mind and a thankful heart.
COLOSSIANS 4:2

Never stop praying.
1 THESSALONIANS 5:17

I urge you, first of all, to pray for all people. Ask God to help them; intercede on their behalf, and give thanks for them. Pray this way for kings and all who are in authority so that we can live peaceful and quiet lives marked by godliness and dignity.
1 TIMOTHY 2:1-2

My fear in listing these texts is that readers will see prayer more as a duty than as a delight. It is a duty because God has commanded it, but it is also a delight because God encourages it. As a new believer in my young teenage years, I prayed only because I knew Christians were supposed to pray. Every Christian I knew prayed at least at church, and most prayed a blessing before a meal.

Our church held a Wednesday night prayer meeting where we added names to a prayer list and prayed for the people on the list. As far as I knew, that was just what believers did.

It wasn't until years later that I learned the unbelievable privilege we have in approaching God in prayer, and it happened through an equipping program designed to teach people to pray. A veteran pastor for whom prayer had become a life-giving, life-sustaining practice led the training, and his love for God permeated his character. When he talked about prayer, I saw joy—even glee—in his eyes. Hearing him pray made me want to pray like he did. Gradually, I came to understand that God commands us to pray because he knows that communicating with him will fill us with delight.

We pray because God works through prayer.

One of my favorite prayer stories in the Bible is the story of Peter's release from prison in Acts 12:6-17. James has just been martyred, but Peter is still alive and in prison in Jerusalem. Meanwhile, the church is praying fervently for him.

Amazingly, Peter was able to sleep the night before he was to go to trial. He was chained to two soldiers until an angel of the Lord miraculously appeared. The scene that unfolds is quite remarkable:

> The angel struck him on the side to awaken him and said, "Quick! Get up!" And the chains fell off his wrists. Then the angel told him, "Get dressed and put on your sandals." And he did. "Now put on your coat and follow me," the angel ordered.
>
> ACTS 12:7-8

Almost step by step, the angel directs Peter out of the prison and leads him through the city gate that miraculously opens on its own. All the while, Peter thinks he is seeing a vision. After all, how often does an angel show up to release you from prison?

Peter eventually comes to his senses and makes his way to the home of Mary, where the believers have been praying. When Peter knocks at the gate, a servant girl recognizes his voice, but she leaves him standing outside while she runs to tell the others that Peter has been released.

The very people who had been praying for Peter thought the servant was out of her mind. Apparently they thought that God would not release Peter even though they were earnestly praying for God's intervention. They assumed that what the servant girl had seen was Peter's angel (Acts 12:15).

The church prayed, and God miraculously answered their prayer. That was a great thing! On the other hand, the church was surprised by God's answer. That is not such a great thing. Too often we respond the same way. We pray for a desired outcome, yet are caught off guard when God answers. But we should not be surprised when he responds to our prayers, because that is the kind of God he is. Our God is a prayer-answering God.

For example, it was in response to prayer that God pulled Lot out of Sodom (Genesis 18–19); gave Hannah a child (1 Samuel 1); granted Solomon wisdom (2 Chronicles 1); brought fire down on the prophets of Baal (1 Kings 18); delivered Hezekiah and his people from the Assyrians (2 Kings 19); extended Hezekiah's life (2 Kings 20); granted Nehemiah favor with the king (Nehemiah 1–2); gave Zechariah and Elizabeth a son as the forerunner of Christ (Luke 1); empowered the early church with boldness (Acts 4); and freed Paul and Silas from prison (Acts 16). Given these stories and others, we cannot miss the truth that God, who established prayer as a means to accomplish his purposes, listens to us when we pray.

Personal Reflection: What is the most significant way God has worked in your life through prayer—either your prayers, the prayers of others, or both?

Prayer slows us down to hear God, trust him, and rest in him.
Some years ago, a study of two hundred pastors and church leaders showed that busyness was the primary reason that churches do not pray.[15] If the church world was busy when that survey was taken, I'm certain we are even busier today. The COVID-19 pandemic that began in 2020 severely limited church activity—for a time. In some ways, the crisis gave churches a rare opportunity to reevaluate their programming and plans. But now as I watch churches restart their ministries, I suspect—and fear—that most will return to busyness as the norm. Churches will once again wear out their members by having too many activities with too little purpose in a world where people are already too busy. And yet we expect believers to find time to pray each day.

It was not without design that Jesus intentionally pushed away from the crowds to pray (Matthew 14:23; Mark 1:35; 6:46; Luke 5:16; 6:12; 9:18). Indeed, these verses show us that Jesus regularly built into his life times of solitude and prayer. He did this partly to get a break from the crowds that were flocking to him as a miracle worker; but more importantly, he prioritized his time with the Father.

When Jesus went away to pray, there were still people who wanted to hear his teachings. Sick people still needed healing. Demoniacs were still under Satan's control. Nonbelievers were still destined for hell. His disciples surely still needed teaching. With so much yet to do, Jesus nevertheless walked away from all the busyness to rest, be quiet, and pray.

Getting away for times of prayer wasn't always easy, either. On at least one occasion, his disciples sought him in his solitude and told him, "Everyone is looking for you" (Mark 1:37).

Sometimes we are so busy that we miss what God is doing around us. Making time for prayer requires us to decrease our busyness (at least temporarily), turn our hearts and minds toward God, and seek refreshment in him. As with many spiritual disciplines, such as Bible study, journaling, silence, and solitude, God uses the practice of prayer to slow us down. He "catches" us when we stop running long enough to do what he wants us to do. If you're at all like me, God may need to catch you to do something mighty in your life.

I find it striking that some of the most prayerful men I know are also some of the most balanced. They are busy, but not so busy that work becomes an idol. They work hard, but they get sufficient rest. They are already wise, yet they find time for ongoing study. They shepherd their families, enjoy their friends, and support their churches—all while finding significant time to pray each day. Most are older, and they have a depth of spiritual zeal and enthusiasm I seldom see in younger men.

Here is what I have learned about these men: Because they prioritize their time in prayer, they steward the rest of their days with wisdom and balance. Even though they have other responsibilities as well, they will not compromise their time with the Father. To get it all done, they have chosen to unclutter their lives and manage their time well—which includes making time to pray. I still have much to learn from these men about discipline and balance.

Sometimes God slows us down and turns our attention to him by delaying his answers to our prayers. In response to our pleas, he may simply tell us, "Wait and trust." The Psalms in particular speak of waiting on the Lord, but this "waiting *on* and *for* the Lord is just the opposite of inactivity; it is a sustained effort of keeping on keeping on in prayer and expectation."[16] For the psalmists, *waiting* meant continuing to seek God even when they could not understand his plan or sense his presence.

As you read the following texts from the Psalms, listen for God-focused confidence and trust even in the midst of waiting. Though God clearly required the psalmists to wait at times, hope still echoes in their words:

Wait patiently for the LORD. Be brave and courageous.
Yes, wait patiently for the LORD.

PSALM 27:14

Be still in the presence of the LORD, and wait patiently for him to act.

PSALM 37:7

For I am waiting for you, O LORD. You must answer for me, O Lord my God.

PSALM 38:15

I waited patiently for the LORD to help me, and he turned to me and heard my cry.

PSALM 40:1

I wait quietly before God, for my victory comes from him. . . . Let all that I am wait quietly before God, for my hope is in him.

PSALM 62:1, 5

> I wait for the LORD, my soul waits, and in his word I
> hope; my soul waits for the Lord more than watchmen
> for the morning, more than watchmen for the morning.
>
> PSALM 130:5-6, ESV

If you're like me, you do not like to wait. When God doesn't answer our prayers as quickly as we would like, our first response is not always to trust God anyway and keep praying. Sometimes we get frustrated with God, struggle with our faith, and neglect prayer—none of which helps, of course.

Waiting reminds us that we are not God. He alone controls the timing of his responses. His clock and calendar are different from ours. His ways are "far beyond" what we can imagine (Isaiah 55:8), and he often uses our times of waiting to do something *within* us in the meantime. God knows his plan. Our responsibility is to trust him in faith even when his ears seem dull. We pray and wait, knowing that God's timing is always right. We genuinely rest in his plan to slow us down and grow our faith by his delayed responses to our prayers.

Prayer encompasses all our Christian life.

The emphasis of our prayers often varies. Some prayers are *petitionary*, asking God to grant us something or do something in our lives. Other prayers are *intercessory*, seeking God's favor on behalf of someone else. Prayers of *praise* honor God for who he is. Prayers of *thanksgiving* express our gratitude to God, and prayers of *confession* admit our sin and seek forgiveness. Then there is meditative prayer, which prayer leader Gregory Frizzell defines as "the act of reflecting on God's Word and quietly listening for His still, small voice."[17]

Praying all these types of prayers is part of living a balanced

Christian life. If we ignore prayers of praise, for example, we may end up focusing too much on self. If we never confess our sins, our relationship with God will be strained and our prayers hindered. If we petition God for our own needs but do not intercede for others, we miss the privilege and responsibility of lifting others in prayer. We also fail to honor God when we don't pray prayers of thanksgiving for his daily blessings. A well-rounded prayer life pushes us upward toward God, inward toward ourselves, and outward toward others.[18]

As we pray for our families and acquaintances, our coworkers and neighbors, our friends and foes, our city and national government leaders, we lift up those who help us and those who hurt us (Luke 6:28). In Ephesians 6:18, the apostle Paul tells us to "Pray in the Spirit at all times and on every occasion. Stay alert and be persistent in your prayers for all believers everywhere." Clearly, prayer is not something we do only occasionally; it envelops our lives.

Prayer strengthens us for the spiritual battle.

Paul was clear about the conflict all believers face: "Put on the whole armor of God, that you may be able to stand against the schemes of the devil. For we do not wrestle against flesh and blood, but against the rulers, against the authorities, against the cosmic powers over this present darkness, against the spiritual forces of evil in the heavenly places" (Ephesians 6:11-12, esv). Indeed, he piles up the phrases describing the enemy's forces to show us they are numerous and powerful; he does not want us to take them lightly.

Our preparation for this conflict is to wear the full armor of God and to pray (Ephesians 6:10-20). Prayer is so central to victory in this battle that we will devote an entire chapter to the topic later in the book.

Making It Personal

Here are some ways to make this chapter personal. You may not use all of them, but perhaps you will find some of these ideas helpful.

One approach is to start a prayer journal that includes not only your prayer requests, but also God's answers to your prayers. If keeping a daily journal seems overwhelming, try journaling once or twice a week. For example, record your prayer concerns on Mondays and review God's answers every Friday.

When God calls you to wait on his response to one of your prayers, enlist another believer (or more) to join you in praying. Pray together, not only for God's answer, but also for the gift of patience as you wait. Somehow, sharing the burden of waiting with others lightens the load.

Another personal application is to ask God to give you a child-like faith as you follow him. Children have a knack for keeping things simple. Your prayer can be short and to the point: "Help me, Lord, to believe in you without reservation today—just like a child does." Pray that way every day for the next week, and let the Lord re-form your heart. When you trust more, you will pray more; and when you pray more, you will trust more.

I encourage you to seek the prayers of other Christians, even as you pray more often for others yourself. With two or three brothers or sisters in Christ, commit to pray for each other daily. Intercede on each other's behalf, even if life seems to be going well. Prayer is for all occasions, not just times of crisis and concern. By covering each other in prayer, we make it difficult for the enemy to gain a foothold in anyone's life.

Be certain to share with your prayer partners and the church all God's answers to your prayers. Some churches create a prayer list and pray for the needs, but they never report what God does in response. By neglecting to share God's answers, they dishonor him and miss a prime opportunity to encourage others to pray. We should all rejoice—in our times of gathered worship and in our small groups—whenever God glorifies himself by answering our prayers. If we believe that prayer makes a difference, we must tell the stories of God's intervention.

Conclusion

Some years ago, when I was working with single adults in local churches, a friend asked me to take her to the airport after a teaching conference. I was happy to oblige, and I looked forward to discussing the conference we had just attended. But when my friend got into the car, she said, "Let's pray aloud on our way to the airport. We can take turns as the Lord leads us." I knew the drive would be about thirty minutes, and I anticipated the trip would be awkward. I had never prayed aloud while driving with a passenger.

To my surprise, the drive was not at all uncomfortable. When my friend began to pray, her personal ease in talking to God quickly became apparent. She spoke to the Lord as if it were just the two of them in the car. It was a tremendous example of *communicating* with God in complete *dependence* on him. My feeble prayers seemed almost like an interruption in a holy moment, but I learned an important lesson that still bears fruit today.

My friend knew that prayer matters. I am still learning that truth. I pray you are too.

Praying like Jesus and the Early Church

I CANNOT HELP but think of the prayer warriors who have influenced my life over the years. Though I didn't always see them as role models for me to emulate at the time, I have since reflected on the example of persistent and passionate prayer they set for me and others.

I think of Sonney and Christie, who prayed regularly for me as their young "preacher boy." From them I learned to see prayer as a *first recourse* rather than a last resort.

I also think of Jim and Ruby, who prayed every day over a lengthy list of names and needs they had written in a spiral-bound notebook. They occasionally invited me to breakfast, but eating was never the primary focus of the morning; intercession was. They also highlighted each prayer request as God answered it, and their notebook was rife with yellow highlighter ink. From them I learned persistence and gratitude.

Tom and Diana pray every day—by name—for every child, grandchild, and great-grandchild in their family (and there are *a lot* of them). They also pray for Pam and me every day. This couple is by far the most praying couple I know, and I am hard-pressed to describe the peace I have knowing that they are praying for me. Simply sharing a prayer concern with them is comforting because I know they will pray about it with intentionality. Tom and Diana have shown me that time is no factor when you commit to praying for others. You find the time to do it because it matters so much.

Others who come to mind include Mrs. Reatherford, who simply trusted God without reservation when she prayed; John, who never misses a day praying for missionaries around the world; Drew, who prays regularly for our leaders at Southeastern Seminary; and my friend D, who prayerfully intercedes for non-believers in a high-security area of the world. With all these role models in mind, however, I realize that not one is a perfect prayer warrior. Only Jesus is perfect, and he is the perfect example for us to emulate as we pray.

As we will see, the early church followed in the prayerful foot-steps of their Master. They, too, had prayer in their DNA. Thus, the goal of this chapter is first to look at Jesus' prayer life, with particular focus on the Gospel of Luke (which records the most stories of Jesus praying). Then we will see how the early church prayed by looking at the book of Acts (which was also written by Luke). My hope is that you will be encouraged and inspired to pray more like Jesus and his early followers.

Personal Reflection: Who are the prayer role models in your life? Have you thanked them for their example?

Jesus Praying in the Gospel of Luke

The theme of prayer reverberates throughout the Gospel of Luke. The book opens with an account of an answered prayer, as an angel appears in the Temple and announces that Zechariah and his wife, Elizabeth, will soon have a son:

> Don't be afraid, Zechariah! God has heard your prayer. Your wife, Elizabeth, will give you a son, and you are to name him John.
>
> LUKE 1:13

Yes, John was the prophesied forerunner of the Messiah, but he was also God's answer to the prayers of an aging, barren couple. God often does amazing things when people pray.

Next, the birth narrative of Jesus includes Simeon's prayer of praise when he holds the Christ child (Luke 2:28-32), and Anna's continual prayer and fasting in the Temple (Luke 2:36-38). These two saints, who had been waiting and praying for God to send the Redeemer, could not help but praise God when Jesus was brought in. Simeon honored God because he could now face death with peace, and Anna announced Jesus in joy to all who had been waiting for him to come. This combination of persistent prayer, heartfelt praise, and gospel proclamation is a good model for all of us.

At the end of Luke's Gospel, stories of Jesus' post-resurrection appearances again emphasize the role of prayer. Though the word *prayer* isn't explicitly used in these accounts, the inference is clear.

In the first story (Luke 24:13-35), Jesus reveals himself to two wearied and burdened disciples on the road to Emmaus. The disciples want him to stay at their home and have a meal. He agrees, and "as they sat down to eat, he took the bread and blessed it" (Luke 24:30), just as he had done when he fed the thousands

(Luke 9:16) and gave his disciples the Last Supper (Luke 22:19). Perhaps it was his familiar prayer over the bread that caused his disciples to recognize him as their resurrected Lord.

The second story (Luke 24:50-51) is the final story in the Gospel of Luke. As Jesus prepares to return to the Father, he lifts up his hands to heaven and blesses his disciples—most assuredly with some kind of prayer. The disciples likely would have recalled their Lord praying over them as one of his final earthly acts before his ascension. We can only wonder how often the disciples might have recalled that blessing in tough times of ministry.

For us, this final story is the bookend to the story of Zechariah and Elizabeth's prayer in Luke 1. Their prayer led to the birth of John, the forerunner of Jesus, and Jesus' prayer in Luke 24 eventually led to his followers carrying the gospel to the ends of the earth. The first prayer paved the way for Jesus to *come*; the second prayer paved the way for his disciples to *go*. In between is a Gospel filled with the prayer life of Jesus.

Jesus serves as our role model for prayer.

We should want to pray like Jesus did; in the words of Andrew Murray, the great nineteenth-century prayer warrior, "Let us this very day say to the Master, as they did of old, 'Lord, teach us to pray.'"[1] Looking at how Jesus prayed in the Gospel of Luke, though, can be overwhelming for those of us who already struggle with prayer.

I offer the list below not to convict you (though the Holy Spirit may have other ideas, even as he did in convicting me as I typed the list), but to show you in summary fashion how often Luke shows us Jesus praying.[2] Review the list, see how often Jesus prayed, and then join me in looking at some particular episodes of Jesus praying.

1. **Jesus prayed as he began his ministry:** "One day when the crowds were being baptized, Jesus himself was baptized. As he was praying, the heavens opened" (Luke 3:21).

2. **He started the day with prayer:** "Early the next morning Jesus went out to an isolated place" (Luke 4:42, cf. Mark 1:35).

3. **He pushed away from the crowds to pray:** "Vast crowds came to hear him preach and to be healed of their diseases. But Jesus often withdrew to the wilderness for prayer" (Luke 5:15-16).

4. **He prayed for followers to invest in:** "One day soon afterward Jesus went up on a mountain to pray, and he prayed to God all night" (Luke 6:12).

5. **He thanked God the Father for food:** "Jesus took the five loaves and two fish, looked up toward heaven, and blessed them" (Luke 9:16).

6. **He spent time praying alone:** "One day Jesus left the crowds to pray alone" (Luke 9:18).

7. **He took others with him on a prayer retreat:** "About eight days later Jesus took Peter, John, and James up on a mountain to pray" (Luke 9:28).

8. **He simply rejoiced in prayer:** "At that same time Jesus was filled with the joy of the Holy Spirit, and he said, 'O Father, Lord of heaven and earth, thank you . . .'" (Luke 10:21).

9. **He taught others how to pray:** "As he finished, one of his disciples came to him and said, 'Lord, teach us to pray, just as John taught his disciples.' Jesus said, 'This is how you should pray'" (Luke 11:1-2).

10. **He prayed for others under spiritual attack:** "Simon, Simon, Satan has asked to sift each of you like wheat.

But I have pleaded in prayer for you, Simon, that your faith should not fail" (Luke 22:31-32).

11. **He cried out to God in his struggle:** "Father, if you are willing, please take this cup of suffering away from me" (Luke 22:42).

12. **He prayed for the Father's will to be done:** "Yet I want your will to be done, not mine" (Luke 22:42).

13. **He prayed for his enemies:** "Father, forgive them, for they don't know what they are doing" (Luke 23:34).

14. **He prayed when he faced death:** "Father, I entrust my spirit into your hands!" (Luke 23:46).

15. **He prayed blessings over his followers:** "Then Jesus led them to Bethany, and lifting his hands to heaven, he blessed them" (Luke 24:50).

In chapter 1, when I talked about getting prayer into the DNA of our churches, I meant making prayer a fundamental commitment or foundation that characterizes the church. Individuals can have that same kind of prayer commitment. Think about people you know who can be identified as *praying people*. Given all we have learned about Jesus' prayer life to this point, it is almost impossible not to see that prayer was an essential part of his spiritual DNA. May we become more like him!

Jesus prayed at his baptism.

If I were to ask most churchgoers what they remember about Jesus' baptism, I suspect many would recall some basic facts. They would know that John the Baptist did the honors, despite his initial reservations. They would also know that the Holy Spirit descended in the form of a dove, and that God the Father spoke from the heavens. What they might *not* recall is the immediate context of all these happenings:

> One day when the crowds were being baptized, Jesus himself was baptized. *As he was praying*, the heavens opened, and the Holy Spirit, in bodily form, descended on him like a dove. And a voice from heaven said, "You are my dearly loved Son, and you bring me great joy."
> LUKE 3:21-22, ITALICS ADDED

Only Luke tells us that these events occurred as Jesus prayed. At the start of his ministry (and at all major turning points in his ministry), Jesus turned to the Father in prayer. Prayer positions us to hear the Father's voice and follow his leading. How much better it is to do that first, rather than the approach we often take: *do* first and then ask God to bless what we have already done.

Jesus prioritized prayer.

On more than one occasion, Luke speaks of Jesus taking time to pray alone (e.g., Luke 6:12; 9:18; 11:1). Luke 4:42 also tells us that Jesus went out to an isolated place, which seems to have been a common practice for him. The text does not directly mention prayer, but the parallel verse in Mark adds that significant detail: "Before daybreak the next morning, Jesus got up and went out to an isolated place to pray" (Mark 1:35). While it was still dark, Jesus sought refuge with the Father away from his disciples and the crowds. He prioritized times of prayer, even if it meant rising very early to do so.

Luke 5:15-16 shows us that Jesus often pushed away from the crowds to pray. Even as people gathered to hear him speak and receive healing from him, he left the busyness and needs behind to go off by himself and pray. Frankly, these are some of the most convicting verses in the Bible for me. If crowds were gathering to hear me preach and people were lying sick before me hoping to receive healing, my desire to minister to them would be so strong that I fear I would plunge headlong into preaching and serving and would pray only if I had time left over. I am enough of a *doer* that leaving people in need "just to pray" would be difficult. But clearly Jesus knew a better way, and we cannot ignore the example of pulling away for prayer that he set for us.

Jesus taught his disciples to pray.

Among the four Gospel writers, Luke alone records that Jesus prayed all night before he called the twelve disciples (Luke 6:12). He had previously encountered some of these young men when they were John's disciples (John 1:35-39), and he had called the fishermen brothers—Peter and Andrew, James and John—to leave their boats behind to follow him (Mark 1:16-20). But Luke tells us that Jesus chose twelve specific men after seeking the Father's direction (Luke 6:12-13). Then he set about teaching them what they needed to know—including how to pray. We learn that as well when we eavesdrop on those conversations Luke recorded.

In Luke 6:28, Jesus teaches his disciples to pray for those who hurt them. This mandate is not an easy one to follow. We all struggle when others have wounded us. Nevertheless, Jesus not only called his followers to pray that way, but he modeled for them how to do it when he prayed for those who were crucifying him (Luke 23:34).

Christ's example always forces me to ask myself, "Who has hurt me, or someone I love, such that I really don't want to pray for them?" Obedience to Christ means that I must ask him for the grace to pray for others as he commanded, including those who have wounded me.

Jesus taught his disciples to pray by modeling prayer for them, but he also intentionally took some of his disciples on at least one prayer retreat (Luke 9:28-36). Only Luke includes the detail that Jesus took Peter, James, and John to the Mount of Transfiguration *to pray.* Just as he pushed away from the crowds at times, he called his followers to do the same. Indeed, it was *as Jesus was praying*—just as at his baptism—that God gloriously brought about the Transfiguration. On the wings of his prayers, Jesus was gloriously changed, and Moses and Elijah appeared. Again, the text reminds us that we sometimes need to step away from busyness and seek the Father if we want to see his work in our lives. It also shows us our responsibility to teach others to do the same.

In Luke 10:1-2, Jesus challenges his followers to pray for more people to spread the gospel even as they themselves are carrying out his work. According to Jesus, the problem isn't that the fields are unripe; it's that there aren't enough workers to bring in the harvest.

So what's the answer?

Prayer.

Jesus instructed the faithful workers to pray that God would raise up more faithful workers. Our process for selecting laborers in our churches may involve more than prayer (e.g., evaluating spiritual giftedness), but it cannot neglect prayer. Neither should the prayer be perfunctory. We must genuinely seek the Father's guidance. The needs of the world are so great that prayer for more laborers is always in order as the church pursues the great commission.

Perhaps the best-known example of how Jesus taught his followers to pray is the model prayer of Luke 11:1-4. There, he taught them to focus on God and his Kingdom (Luke 11:2), to seek his daily blessings (Luke 11:3), and to request forgiveness for sin and protection from temptation (Luke 11:4). His followers were to approach God as "Father"—a most unique familial, relational understanding in the first-century world—and trust that he who loved them would also provide for them. After all, if men as evil fathers still give good gifts to their children, God as the perfect Father grants the greater gift of his Holy Spirit (Luke 11:5-13). In essence, Jesus was asking his disciples (and *us*, by extension), "Why would you *not* seek the Father when you have needs?" God provides for us, but even more significantly, he gives himself to us.

The setting of this prayer teaching in Luke 11 and the content of its message lead me to ask four questions about your prayer life (and my own, for that matter).

First, if I were to be with you every moment for the next week—going everywhere you go, doing everything you do—would I be inclined at the end of the week to ask you to teach me to pray like you do? In other words, would you be happy if I were to model my prayer life after yours? I daresay not many would answer *yes* to that question.

Second, how much attention do you give to God's holiness when you pray? I have heard many prayers that immediately go to the problem while leaping over or ignoring God, who is the answer to the problem. We start our prayers more with "Help me" than with "Father, may your name be kept holy" (Luke 11:2). When our focus in prayer is more on ourselves than on God, we give evidence that we do not fully understand what prayer is. Prayer is simply communicating with God, but it *matters* who God is. It is a marvelous grace that allows sinful people like you and me to approach a perfectly holy God with boldness (Hebrews 4:16).

Third, who has the privilege of seeing and hearing you pray? The disciples wanted to pray as Jesus prayed because they had seen and heard him pray. They had previously learned prayer as a *ritual* (that is, they learned the routine of prayer in Judaism), but Jesus showed them both *relationship* and *results.* Prayer was not just a spiritual discipline for him; it was an essential part of who he was. It's possible that hearing Jesus pray (Luke 9:18) caught his disciples' attention to the extent that they asked him to teach them how (Luke 11:1-13). Listening to Jesus pray made them want to pray more effectively.

Who, then, sees and hears you pray? My concern is that if we always retreat to a quiet place to pray on our own, our children and grandchildren may not know that we ever pray without a meal in front of us. Secluding ourselves to pray is, of course, both biblical (Matthew 6:6) and necessary at times, but let us not miss the opportunity to model prayer for our families. My students today who are most faithful in their spiritual disciplines tend to come from Christian homes where their parents openly spent time with God. They remember seeing open Bibles and hearing the prayers of their parents, and they want to be like them. If you are a parent or grandparent (or aunt or uncle, for that matter), I encourage you to let others see and hear you pray.

Fourth, how do you pray about temptation? Jesus was clear about how we ought to pray: "Don't let us yield to temptation" (Luke 11:4). Matthew expands that prayer to include "but rescue us from the evil one" (Matthew 6:13), but both passages emphasize one truth: We are to seek God's protection from the evil one *before* we face temptation. That is also the way Jesus pushed his disciples to pray in the garden of Gethsemane: "Pray that you will not give in to temptation" (Luke 22:40).

For too many Christians, praying about temptation happens not *before* it comes, nor even *during* the temptation, when it might do some good. Rather, they often pray only *after* the temptation, when seeking forgiveness for sinning again. Maybe we would live more godly lives if we prayed about temptation the way Jesus taught us to pray. We must pray proactively, not reactively. We mustn't wait until we are under attack before we seek God's help.

Given the corporate nature of the model prayer, it seems only wise to secure other believers to pray for us too. How much better to rally some prayer partners to help us *avoid* the devil's trap, rather than waiting until we've failed and then calling for help to get off the ground and receive God's forgiveness. Proactively seek others who will intercede for you. You will not regret gathering that prayer team around you.

Jesus not only taught his disciples to pray, but he also urged them to pray with persistence. Prior to recording Jesus' parable of the persistent widow (Luke 18:2-8), Luke also notes that Jesus spoke this parable so that the disciples "should always pray and never give up" (Luke 18:1). Trying days lay ahead, with Jesus' arrest and crucifixion. Later, the disciples would face religious and political persecution as they led the nascent church. Jesus knew they would be tempted to quit praying, and he challenged them to stay on their knees before God.

Jesus' own example of praying under pressure would also remind his disciples to pray when it might be easy to give up. In the most gripping moments in the garden of Gethsemane, Jesus poured out his heart to the Father (Luke 22:39-46). At the same time, he reminded his disciples again to pray lest they fall into temptation (Luke 22:40, 46). He also prayed for his murderers as they gambled away his garments (Luke 23:34), and he prayed with his final breath (Luke 23:46). On the mountaintop or in the valley, Jesus kept on praying. Even today, he intercedes for his followers (Romans 8:34; Hebrews 7:25) as his ministry of prayer continues.

I am struck by the fact that Jesus' disciples were tempted to quit praying and give up. I understand why that would be, but I also know they had learned to pray at the feet of the Master prayer warrior. They could have found no greater role model. Apparently, though, prayer can be difficult even for those who learned directly from Jesus. In a strange way, I find comfort in this text; if Jesus' closest disciples struggled to maintain their prayer life, you and I are likely to battle that tendency too. Maybe Christ's example of persistence under pressure will help us fight to remain faithful in praying like he did.

Personal Reflection: Which of these teachings about Jesus' prayer life is most convicting to you? What steps might you take to change your prayer life as a result?

The Early Church Praying in the Book of Acts

The book of Acts includes several summaries of the growth of the early church that are quite convicting to me as a pastor. I long for my church to grow, and I believe the Lord can accomplish it, but I don't always pray with faith that the God who grew the early church in unusual ways will do the same today.

Review with me these summary statements about the growth of the church in Acts (and be prepared to have them humble you):

- **Acts 2:41** – Those who believed . . . were baptized and added to the church that day—about 3,000 in all.

- **Acts 2:47** – *Each day* the Lord added to their fellowship those who were being saved. (Italics added.)

- **Acts 4:4** – Many of the people who heard their message believed it, so the number of men who believed now totaled about 5,000.

- **Acts 5:14** – More and more people believed and were brought to the Lord—crowds of both men and women.

- **Acts 6:7** – God's message continued to spread. The number of believers greatly increased in Jerusalem, and many of the Jewish priests were converted, too.

- **Acts 9:31** – The church then had peace throughout Judea, Galilee, and Samaria, and it became stronger as the believers lived in the fear of the Lord. And with the encouragement of the Holy Spirit, it also grew in numbers.

- **Acts 11:21-22, 24** – The power of the Lord was with them, and a large number of these Gentiles believed and turned to the Lord. When the church at Jerusalem heard what had happened, they sent Barnabas to Antioch. . . . And many people were brought to the Lord.

- **Acts 16:5** – The churches were strengthened in their faith and grew larger every day.

- **Acts 19:20** – The message about the Lord spread widely and had a powerful effect.

- **Acts 28:31** – [In Rome, Paul was] boldly proclaiming the Kingdom of God and teaching about the Lord Jesus Christ. *And no one tried to stop him.* (Italics added.)

When you consider that at least 65 percent of churches in North America today are either plateaued or declining, it is hard to fathom the kind of growth the early church experienced in decidedly hostile surroundings.[3] Those early Christians lived God-honoring lives (even unto death), preached the Word, and prayed like Jesus prayed. Indeed, just as prayer is evident throughout the Gospel of Luke, it is equally evident throughout the book of Acts, Luke's follow-up to his Gospel. My former professor, New Testament scholar John Polhill, summarizes it this way: "Prayer was a hallmark of the church in its early days."[4]

Walk with me through Luke's record. The early believers gathered for a time of prayer in Acts 1:14 as they awaited the coming of the Spirit, and they continually devoted themselves to prayer in the life of the young church (Acts 2:42). When they faced major decisions, such as replacing the traitor Judas (Acts 1:24) or setting apart missionaries (Acts 13:1-3), they prayed. In the power of prayer, they saw Samaritans filled with the Spirit (Acts 8:14-17), Dorcas resurrected (Acts 9:36-43), Peter freed from prison (Acts 12:1-19), and Publius's father healed (Acts 28:7-8). So important was prayer to them that they selected servant helpers to free up the apostles to focus on praying and preaching; then, the apostles prayed over these men as they put them to work (Acts 6:1-6).

To summarize about the early church and prayer: "When they were fearful, they prayed. When they were confused, they prayed. When they were waiting for God to fulfill his promise to them, they prayed. When they needed an answer to a question (such as who was to be the twelfth apostle), they prayed!"[5] The early believers were a bunch of common people who lived in the power of God through a lifestyle of consistent prayer.

Much of the prayer in the early church was directly connected to pursuing the great commission. As opposition grew, the church turned to God in prayer. The apostles continued to proclaim what they had seen and heard, even after being warned (Acts 4:17-20), and the other believers prayed for them to continue to speak with boldness. So potent was their prayer that "the meeting place shook" under divine power (Acts 4:31), perhaps like an earthquake. God was with these Christians, and he immediately empowered them through a fresh filling of the Holy Spirit to speak the Word of God boldly.

Personal Reflection: Have you ever been in a prayer meeting where the power of God was powerfully evident? Do you need a fresh filling of the Spirit today?

As Paul and his church-planting team carried the gospel throughout the Roman empire, prayer was central to their efforts. It was not a coincidence that the church in Antioch was praying and fasting when the Holy Spirit directed them to set apart Paul and Barnabas for the first missionary journey (Acts 13:1-3). The believers had been seeking God expectantly and ardently, so much so that even eating did not matter to them. They needed God's guidance, and the Spirit provided that direction. The church set apart Paul and Barnabas and then prayed and fasted some more—surely to ask God's blessing on the work of the missionaries.

Paul followed the same pattern of prayer and fasting as he interceded for elders he and his team appointed in each city (Acts 14:23). Then, as he left those cities, he often wept and prayed with the elders as he said his farewells (Acts 20:36-37; 21:5). In God's power and in the strength of Paul's prayers, they would continue the work. That work eventually cost Paul his life; and though the believers in Ephesus would never see him again, their final memory of Paul was one of heartfelt prayer.

The book of Acts describes Paul's missionary journeys, but his corresponding writings more clearly reflect his commitment to prayer for himself and for others. For example, he prayed with perseverance for the believers:

I have not stopped thanking God for you. I pray for you constantly.

EPHESIANS 1:16

Every time I think of you, I give thanks to my God.

PHILIPPIANS 1:3

We always pray for you.

COLOSSIANS 1:3

We keep on praying for you.

2 THESSALONIANS 1:11

At the same time, Paul sought prayer from those same believers:

I urge you in the name of our Lord Jesus Christ to join in my struggle by praying to God for me.

ROMANS 15:30

You are helping us by praying for us.

2 CORINTHIANS 1:11

Pray for me, too. Ask God to give me the right words so I can boldly explain God's mysterious plan that the Good News is for Jews and Gentiles alike.

EPHESIANS 6:19

I know that as you pray for me and the Spirit of Jesus Christ helps me, this will lead to my deliverance.

PHILIPPIANS 1:19

Pray for us, too, that God will give us many opportunities
to speak. . . . Pray that I will proclaim this message as
clearly as I should.

COLOSSIANS 4:3-4

We ask you to pray for us. Pray that the Lord's message
will spread rapidly and be honored wherever it goes. . . .
Pray, too, that we will be rescued from wicked and evil
people.

2 THESSALONIANS 3:1-2

Paul knew he could never fulfill God's great commission apart
from God's power. Neither could the other believers—so Paul
prayed and called them to join him in praying.

Marvelous conversion stories in Acts are also wrapped in prayer.
For example, Cornelius was praying when an angel directed him
to Peter to hear the gospel (Acts 10:1-8, 30-33). At the same time,
Peter was praying when God gave him his vision of a sheet coming
from heaven—a vision revealing that the gospel was for all people
(Acts 10:9-15). Though the church would still debate whether
Gentiles should be included in their number, God had made his
plans clear when two men prayed in different places.

In Acts 9, Saul of Tarsus is praying when God sends Ananias to
him to restore his sight and set him apart as God's "chosen instru-
ment to take my message to the Gentiles and to kings, as well as
to the people of Israel" (Acts 9:15). As Gary Millar describes this
scene in *Calling on the Name of the Lord*, "In context this does
not simply imply that Saul is engaged in general religious activity
(which, of course, had been part of his life for many years as an
observant Jew). This must mean that he is 'calling on the name of
the Lord,' asking for mercy in the face of his recent actions and

lifelong pride."[6] Saul was praying because the Lord had grabbed his heart.

Moreover, prayer sustained the persecuted believers in the book of Acts. Prayer brought Peter's release from prison, but those who were praying for him had to be convinced it really was Peter when he arrived at their door (Acts 12:1-19). Paul and Silas in the Philippian jail were apparently not burdened by their imprisonment; instead, they sang and prayed to God as the other prisoners listened to them—and those prisoners even stayed in the jail to hear more of the Word after an earthquake opened the prison doors (Acts 16:25-34). Stephen, the first martyr of the early church, died as his Lord did: praying for those who were killing him and committing his spirit to the Lord (Acts 7:54-60).

To live and die with prayer on our lips—that ought to be our desire and commitment. Prayer was at the heart of the early church, as the following list reminds us.[7]

Acts 1:14 – The early believers were united in prayer.

Acts 1:24 – They prayed to determine Judas's replacement.

Acts 2:42 – They devoted themselves to prayer.

Acts 4:29-31 – They prayed for boldness in the midst of opposition.

Acts 6:4-6 – The apostles focused on prayer and then prayed for newly selected servants.

Acts 7:54-60 – Stephen prayed as he was martyred.

Acts 8:15 – They prayed for the Samaritans to receive the Holy Spirit.

Acts 9:11 – Saul was praying as he awaited Ananias.

Acts 9:40 – Peter prayed for Tabitha's resurrection.

Acts 10:9 – Peter was praying when he received his vision.

Acts 10:1-8, 30-33 – Cornelius was also praying.

Acts 12:5 – The church prayed for Peter's release from prison.

Acts 13:3 – The Antioch church prayed for Paul and Barnabas as they sent them out.

Acts 14:23 – Paul and Barnabas prayed for elders they appointed.

Acts 16:16 – Paul and Silas met a demon-possessed girl on their way to prayer.

Acts 16:25 – Paul and Silas prayed in the Philippian jail.

Acts 20:36 – Paul prayed with the Ephesian elders as he left them.

Acts 21:5 – Paul and his team prayed for disciples in Tyre.

Acts 22:17 – Paul prayed in the Temple.

Acts 28:8 – Paul prayed for Publius's father and healed him.

The early church was born in prayer and lived in prayer, and its members died in prayer. Wouldn't it be something if church historians could someday describe the contemporary church in North America with those same words? As it stands, my guess is that the early church (and many prayer-saturated believers around the world today) would not understand the prayerlessness of the North American church. At the same time, I agree with John Onwuchekwa, who says that the biggest problem with prayer in most churches is "not a complete lack of prayer, but too little prayer."[8] I have not yet encountered a church that never prays at all, but I have known many who do not pray much.

Here is an immediate, real-life illustration that has suddenly presented itself.

I just noticed that the power supply on my laptop is getting low. I have been writing for hours, working on this chapter. My focus has been on word after word, sentence after sentence, paragraph after paragraph, and section after section. I have been "in the zone," and I have not paused to do anything else.

However, my computer has been slowly dying. The power adapter is lying on the floor next to me—ready to be plugged in—but I have been so wrapped up in the task that I overlooked my waning power supply. All the while, more than sufficient power has been easily within my reach.

It strikes me that we lead our lives and guide our churches in much the same way. We are so focused on the task at hand, so goal-oriented, so busy, and so absorbed in our work that we don't realize our batteries are running low. A more-than-sufficient—one might say *overabundant*—power supply is readily available, but we are disconnected from the source. We'll go as far as we can, plugging in sporadically—that is, it's not that we *never* pray—but over time our power will inevitably and inexorably dissipate because we pray too little. In many cases, God sovereignly brings us to the end of ourselves or raises up someone else who reads our situation better than we do to show us our prayer deficiency.

Making It Personal

If you felt inadequate to pray before reading this chapter, you may not feel any better now. But there are some immediate and practical ways to apply this chapter to your life. For example, take some time to humbly share with another person what you are learning about prayer. Just like Jesus taught his disciples to pray, help someone else pray. Learn together. If that someone is your child or grandchild, that's a great way to influence the next generations.

As a church member, enlist a few other believers to join you in regular times of prayer. These may be the same prayer partners you sought after reading chapter 2, or they may be a different group entirely. Step away from the busyness of life and spend 30–60 minutes in prayer each week. Historically, God has ignited great spiritual awakenings through the prayers of a few people, and he might choose to do the same through you and some believing friends. Call on the name of the Lord together.

Perhaps your congregation would study together the texts from Luke and Acts that we've looked at in this chapter. It's one thing to simply read the verses; but digesting them in a corporate Bible study could take your understanding and practice of prayer to a whole new level. If you're a pastor, consider preaching a sermon series on these texts. If you're a layperson, humbly talk to your pastor about teaching these truths.

However you choose to study these texts, keep in mind that intellectual study will take you only so far if you don't also fall on your knees. You might understand Luke's writings better, but little will change unless you prioritize prayer. Plan it into your life and daily routine, and always be ready to erupt in prayer when you have opportunity to praise the Lord or seek his grace. Remember: The goal is to make prayer part of your (and your church's) spiritual DNA.

Lighting the Fire

I am a former volunteer firefighter. From that experience, I know the amazing potential of a spark or an ember. A huge conflagration can ignite from the tiniest combination of fuel, heat, and oxygen.

Sometimes the young flame will spread slowly at first. Sometimes it will grow behind a wall before it becomes evident. Sometimes the first evidence is only a plume of smoke, but that plume indicates that something is happening.

It might be that you and your church have just a spark of prayer happening right now. People are praying, but it's more behind the scenes and few members know the role it plays in your congregation. But even if that is the case, thank God for the spark and commit to helping the fire grow. The flame may increase one person at a time, one family at a time, one small group at a time, one congregation at a time—but an oxygenated flame with sufficient heat and fuel *will* grow.

I am praying that this book will help you stay connected to your power supply through prayer. And I am praying that the embers of your flame will produce a blaze of prayer in others.

4

The Battle of Prayer

I HAVE A confession to make that might surprise you: I am a fan of old-fashioned professional wrestling. I grew up watching it every Saturday afternoon with my saintly grandma. "Rasslin'" is what she called it, and we never missed it. Watching "rasslin'" on Grandma's black-and-white television was as normal as having lunch together—which we did every Saturday a few hours before the matches began.

For the most part, we knew who the "good guys" and "bad guys" were. Heroes and villains. Sometimes they changed roles—a switch that often visibly upset my grandma—but the battle was always good versus evil. When evil won, it was almost always a temporary victory before the good guys regained the crown. Perseverance in good usually won the day, even when the battle to get there included (or at least appeared to include) chaotic conflicts with uncertain endings.

The battles we'll discuss in this chapter are hardly the orchestrated conflicts of the pro wrestling circuit; rather, they are real and intense confrontations, with real consequences, against a real and ruthless enemy. There is nothing fake about the enemy who attacks God and his church. The victory is certain—that is, Jesus has already disarmed the powers through his work on the cross (Colossians 2:15)—but the battle is nonetheless real. In God's unique plan, his people find victory in him while living on their knees in prayer and proclaiming the good news of salvation to a dying world.

"Prayer is the heart of spiritual warfare,"[1] and it's not easy. If it were, we wouldn't need books teaching us how to do it. Prayer itself is a battle within a much larger battle, and it's likely the most difficult spiritual discipline to master. I know that from my own experience, and maybe you've been there too. If not, you probably will be at some point.

My goal in this chapter is to help you see why prayer is often so difficult. When we understand the causes behind our struggles with prayer, we are more likely to overcome them. We will be better prepared to pray individually and corporately.

Reasons for the Struggle

I have spent many years talking to students and pastors about their walk with God. Most often, I hear about their desire to pray more and to pray more effectively. Based on these conversations, here are my general conclusions about why we struggle with prayer:

1. **Leaders are "fixers" by nature.** We are problem solvers who seek solutions, attempt answers, and try again if the first answer doesn't work. Our persistence and determination to solve problems—both good traits in themselves—sometimes push prayer to a last-resort

option. We pray only when all else fails, and we tend not to pray if we can accomplish things on our own.

2. **We never learned how to pray.** As noted before, churches make the same mistake with many of the spiritual disciplines: We tell believers *what* they should do, but we don't teach them *how* to do it. If we're honest as leaders, we have to admit that we, too, have much to learn about how to pray. But pride keeps us from telling anyone.

3. **Prayer has become more about ritual than about relationship.** We know we should pray, even if we don't know how, so we go through the motions. Instead of pursuing an active relationship with a living Lord who calls us to pray, we lapse into a religious ritual. In some cases, we pray more in a formal church setting than we do in private.

4. **Prayerlessness can be hidden.** We can *talk* about prayer, *teach* about prayer, *write* about prayer, and even *lead* corporately in prayer—all without anyone knowing that our personal prayer life is sporadic at best.

5. **Sin keeps us from praying.** It is difficult to approach God in prayer when we have unconfessed sin in our lives. After all, how can we talk to God as if nothing is wrong when something is very wrong? Even praying a prayer of confession can sometimes be difficult when guilt and shame have consumed us.

6. **We don't believe prayer works.** No church leader I know would teach that prayer is ineffective. We can't help but talk about the power of prayer if we teach the stories of the Bible. But our own prayer lives often suggest that we don't really believe in its power. Sometimes we struggle with believing, but we are unwilling to admit it.

7. **We have never been broken under God's hand.** The apostle Paul, who was a leader extraordinaire, learned the power of strength in weakness (2 Corinthians 12:7-10). It is in our weakness that we learn how to pray; but as leaders we naturally fight against weakness. In fact, we are trained not to show weakness. We will talk more about this topic in chapter 5.

8. **Leaders read the Bible in a one-sided way.** We have previously talked about the importance of connecting our Bible reading with our praying. Leaders, though, are often teachers who read God's Word for information transmission more than life transformation. When we approach Scripture that way, we miss the opportunity to be in dialogue with God.

9. **Some leaders have simply lost hope.** It happens. Ministry can be difficult. Life can be hard. Church leaders who once prayed frequently sometimes lose hope under the weight of church conflict, family struggles, or health concerns. Unanswered prayer leads to faithlessness, which leads to prayerlessness.

10. **We have no role models.** Too many Christians— including Christian leaders—have never met a genuine prayer warrior. I have already mentioned some prayer warriors I have been privileged to know, but they are few and far between. Sadly, it's difficult to find people who really pray.

11. **We do not have God-sized goals.** Some years ago, a friend challenged me with this question: "What are you trying to do in your life that only God can do?" I must admit I had nothing to say at that point in my life. I was involved in ministry, but doing nothing extraordinary.

Only when we try to accomplish something far beyond our own abilities do we pray ferociously. Even leaders sometimes put a limit on our expectations.

12. **Prayer is a spiritual battle.** We struggle with prayer because our supernatural, evil enemy does not want us to pray.[2]

The relationship between spiritual warfare and prayer is the topic of the rest of this chapter. Before we move forward, I encourage you to take a minute to pray that the enemy will not hinder your learning about this battle.

Personal Reflection: Which of the twelve reasons reflects why you do not always pray like you should? What is your plan to overcome that obstacle?

The Battle in the Heavens

Let me take you to a behind-the-scenes story in the Bible that is quite fascinating (Daniel 9–10). The prophet Daniel is with God's people in Babylon, where they have been exiled for almost seventy years because of their sin. While reading the book of Jeremiah, Daniel realizes their captivity is coming to an end. He begins to fast and pray, asking God for the restoration of his people.

Daniel's prayer is a good model to follow. He begins by recognizing who God is (Daniel 9:4), follows by confessing the people's sin (Daniel 9:4-15), and then appeals for God to intervene on their behalf (Daniel 9:16-19). Throughout his prayer, he recognizes that God is "in the right" (Daniel 9:7) to do what he had done in judgment. Nevertheless, he pleads for God's undeserved mercy on behalf of his people who bear his name, and he does it with heartfelt passion and great urgency:

O our God, hear your servant's prayer!

DANIEL 9:17

O my God, lean down and listen to me.

DANIEL 9:18

O Lord, hear. O Lord, forgive. O Lord, listen and act!
For your own sake, do not delay, O my God.

DANIEL 9:19

God answers Daniel's prayer by sending the angel Gabriel to
him with a message. In this case, the Lord miraculously responds
to the prophet's prayer without delay.

Sometime later, in another time of distress, Daniel has been
mourning for three weeks when he sees a vision of an angel from
God (perhaps Gabriel, according to Daniel 9:21). So overwhelming is the vision that Daniel faints, but the angel lifts Daniel and
offers him hope. God heard Daniel's prayer, the angel said, but a
twenty-one day battle in the heavens had delayed God's response.
An evil force known as "the spirit prince of the kingdom of Persia"
(Daniel 10:13) blocked the response until the angel Michael
showed up. Michael battled against the king of Persia and freed
the angel to bring an encouraging word to Daniel.

Daniel's prayer had made it to heaven, but conflict between
forces in the heavenlies had delayed the response. All the time that
Daniel had been praying, a supernatural battle had been under-
way; but no power could ultimately stop God from answering the
prophet's prayer. No power is greater than God.

Though we have only one specific biblical example of this kind
of battle, Daniel's story reveals a connection between prayer and
spiritual warfare. When we seek God, the enemy is not pleased. He

doesn't like it when we confess our love for God and our dependence on him as we pray.

On one hand, Satan and his forces want to entice us not to pray at all. They delight when we operate in our own power and for our own glory; they are not alarmed by all our church programs as long as we lack the power of God in what we do. Daniel, of course, was not a prayerless man. He prayed *a lot*. Three times a day, in fact (Daniel 6:10). He was, without question, "a man of prayer and . . . an example of the importance of that discipline for modern believers."[3]

On the other hand, at times the enemy apparently fights against our receiving God's answer to our prayers. We don't know when such a battle might be happening—Daniel didn't know until the angel told him—but we must keep praying nonetheless, knowing that God is faithful. And this is why *waiting on God* in prayer is so important. Knowing that the enemy fights against us, and that he particularly wants to discourage us when God's response to our prayers is not immediate should inspire us to persevere in prayer.

Maybe my own story will help you understand this battle and encourage you at the same time. I was not raised in a Christian home. I knew nothing of the gospel until a twelve-year-old classmate told me about Jesus. He was aggressive in his evangelism, and God called me to himself and made me his child when I was thirteen. My life hasn't been the same since then.

My first pastor told me I should immediately start telling others about Jesus and praying for them to respond in faith. I started praying for my parents, neither of whom had been raised in church. I prayed with excitement and expectation. I was sure they would want to experience what I had experienced and they would turn to Jesus. Little did I know that I would pray for *decades* before my parents came to faith in Christ. Actually, it was thirty-six years for my dad and forty-seven for my mom.

They had both heard the gospel and fought against it for years, but God eventually grabbed their hearts. And when it happened—more than a decade apart—both were so changed by the transforming power of the gospel that we almost didn't recognize them.

Wonder satisfied their questions. Peace trumped their fears. Joy replaced anger. Love overtook bitterness. Smiles won out over frowns and sadness. Childlike faith marked their lives, even in their seventies. My dad went to be with the Lord three years after his salvation, and the peace in his eyes when he died became an undeniable witness to my mom for years thereafter. In fact, my mom spoke of that same peace not long before she passed away.

I would be lying, though, if I told you I always trusted, always believed, always looked forward in faith to my parents becoming believers. There were times when my prayers were burning, but there were other times when they were waning. Sometimes I wept; sometimes I felt no emotion at all. I got discouraged more often than I care to admit. At times it was a battle to keep praying, and I sometimes wondered whether God was even listening. My faith increased when my dad became a Christian, but the eleven years between his conversion and my mom's stretched my faith yet again. I'm convinced the enemy was doing all he could to keep me from praying—and, truthfully, only the grace and mercy of God kept me on my knees.

But that's the answer when the enemy tries to discourage us about waiting: Keep praying anyway. In fact, one of the reasons the enemy attacks us when we pray is because prayer is such a powerful and effective weapon against his schemes.

Personal Reflection: How much do you trust God when the situation requires you to wait? Do you wrestle with wanting to give up on prayer?

So why *does* the enemy fight against prayer? First, prayer says, "God, I love you" and "God, I need you." Satan and his forces do not like either one of those ideas. They detest our relationship with God and our dependence on him. They much prefer it when our actions degrade our love for God and our independence rejects any notion that we need him.

Second, prayer is an act of faith. Prayer says not only, "I love you and need you," but also, "I trust that you can grant me triumph over the enemy. I believe you are working on my behalf even if I cannot see you." Prayer sees victory even in the tragedy of a wooden cross, the grief of a borrowed tomb, the pain of political and religious persecution, and the intensity of spiritual conflict; it seeks God in the midst of the battle and finds hope there. Evil forces cannot stand against such hope.

Third, prayer is powerful against everything the enemy wants to accomplish. He wants to deceive us, but prayer turns us to the truth. He wants us to give in to temptation, but prayer seeks victory through Christ. He wants to keep nonbelievers in darkness, but God works through prayer to rescue them. Satan may be powerful, but God is all-powerful, and the Almighty One has ordained prayer as the means to communicate with him. Satan wants to rob God of his glory, but believers on their knees in prayer bring God glory.

Prayer as Preparation for Battle

Let me start by reminding you of the importance of praying *proactively*. If we wait until the enemy has already won a battle, our praying starts too late. Both Jesus and Paul taught us to pray in *preparation* for the battle. We will briefly review Jesus' teaching and then focus on Paul's teaching about prayer and the armor of God.

Jesus: "Deliver us from the evil one."

In the model prayer Jesus gave us, he directs us to pray that the Father will deliver us from the evil one. Jesus certainly knew the force of the enemy's temptations, for he had faced his own battle at the beginning of his ministry (Matthew 4:1-11). The same enemy who was brazen enough to attack Jesus will certainly come after his followers, and Jesus wants us to be ready for the attack. Preparation means praying to the Father for his protection.

I love how one writer describes God's help: "God can deliver the believer from Satan's temptation by giving the alertness to recognize it, the wisdom to avoid it, and the grace to conquer it."[4] All God's help comes when we pray. Unfortunately, the opposite is also true: When we *don't* pray, we are not alert to temptation, we do not have the wisdom to flee it, and we hardly rely on God's grace. In temptation, prayerlessness equals defeat.

If you do not already pray for deliverance from the evil one, I encourage you to make it a regular habit as soon as you wake up in the morning. Before you ever put your feet on the floor, ask God to guard you. Seek his power and his grace to stand strong against the enemy's arrows of temptation. The longer into the day you wait to utter that prayer, the more likely it is that the enemy will gain a victory somewhere. When temptation comes (and it will), pray for deliverance from the evil one as soon as you recognize the struggle. As you turn to God and rely on him for deliverance from evil, he will grant you victory.

As an illustration, the command we're given in James 4:7-8 to fight against the enemy reflects the same teaching from Jesus:

"Humble yourselves before God. Resist the devil, and he will flee from you. Come close to God, and God will come close to you." Some teachers and writers on the topic of spiritual warfare give more attention to resisting the devil than to submitting to God, but that is not the priority established by James. He says that victory over Satan begins with humbling ourselves before God, a phrase translated as "submit yourselves to God" in some Bible versions (e.g., ESV). When we run to God, place ourselves under his authority, and trust him to stand against the enemy, the enemy flees because he cannot win against God.

Moreover, we are to *come close* to God. Like the priests in the Old Testament who prepared themselves for worship and sacrifice, Christians are called to turn away from our wrongdoing and "draw near" to God (ESV). This process of approaching God involves more than just praying, but it certainly includes seeking God in prayer. In prayer, we confess our sins and seek God's deliverance from the enemy's temptations.

Personal Reflection: How well do you resist the devil in prayer? When facing temptation, do you flee to God and seek his help?

Jesus not only taught us to pray for deliverance from the evil one, he also modeled that kind of praying. In his high priestly prayer in John 17, he prays for his followers: "I'm not asking you to take them out of the world, but to keep them safe from the evil one" (John 17:15). Satan seeks to deceive Jesus' followers and destroy their ministry before they ever start, but Jesus prays against that possibility. The enemy will still attack, and his forces will assault us with a vengeance, but we know that Jesus has already prayed for us. Certainly his words should strengthen us even though we often struggle in the battle.

Moreover, Jesus also asked his Father to sanctify his followers: "Make them holy by your truth; teach them your word, which is truth" (John 17:17). Jesus asked his Father to set apart his followers, characterizing them as holy and preparing them for the mission to which he had called them—a mission that will include spiritual conflict. Through God's work in our lives, we will love God, love his Word, know his Word, and live out his Word as truth. We will "do only what God wants, and hate all that God hates. That is what it means to be holy, as God is holy."[5] Through the truth of God's Word, believers stand *for* God and against the enemy.

Jesus also prayed for Simon Peter when Satan requested permission to "sift" him and the other disciples "like wheat" (Luke 22:31-32). It is good news that Satan could not attack the disciples without God's permission; but it's also humbling to know that God grants him permission at times. The better news is that Jesus never leaves us alone in the battle; he who allows the enemy to attack us also prays us through the conflict. His prayers lead to our victory.

In Peter's case, the arrows the enemy aimed at his heart hit their mark, and Peter denied knowing Christ three times. What he did *not* do, however, was ultimately reject his allegiance to Jesus. We know he wept bitterly over his sin (Luke 22:62), was restored to fellowship by Jesus (John 21:15-17), and would later lead the disciples again (Acts 2:14-41). Peter fell temporarily, but Satan did not ultimately win. Once Jesus had pleaded in prayer for Simon Peter—*before* the attack—Satan's fate was sealed.

What, then, is Jesus doing for us now? He is interceding on our behalf as our advocate with the Father (Romans 8:34; Hebrews 7:25; 1 John 2:1). Satan may try to condemn us, but Christ stands for us on the basis of his atoning death in our place. He has already won the war. You and I live in victory, not only because of Jesus' death and resurrection, but also because of his ongoing intercessory ministry.

Paul: "Be persistent in your prayers."

A number of years ago, I cowrote a study on spiritual warfare that included video-recorded teachings to accompany the lessons.[6] In one of the recordings, my cowriter and I stood next to a life-size suit of armor in an old castle and explained the armor of God as the apostle Paul describes it in Ephesians 6:13-17. The suit of armor we used did not look like the armor a Roman soldier would have worn in the first century, but it helped us visualize the pieces of armor as we taught about them. I have found New Testament scholar Clinton Arnold's descriptions of the armor helpful—particularly the recognition that prayer is the bottom line:

1. **Put On Your Trousers: Wear Truth.** Know the truth of who you are in Christ (for the powers of darkness will try to deceive you). Practice honesty and live with moral integrity.
2. **Put On the Breastplate of Righteousness.** Realize your status before God as one who has been acquitted of all guilt. Acquire personal holiness and develop good character.
3. **Put On Your Boots: Prepare to Share the Gospel of Peace.** Prepare yourself for sharing the gospel wherever God calls you.
4. **Take the Shield of Faith.** Do not doubt! Believe that God will help you overcome.
5. **Put On the Helmet of Salvation.** Be secure in your identity in Christ—as one who has been saved, united with Christ, made alive, co-resurrected, and co-exalted.

6. **Take the Sword of the Spirit, the Word of God.** Devote your life to aggressively spreading the gospel. Know Scripture and apply it to every difficult situation.

7. **The Bottom Line: Pray!** Ask God to strengthen you and other believers to resist temptation and share the gospel effectively.[7]

Look again at the last item above. Prayer really does matter in spiritual warfare. In fact, Paul's words reflect a great sense of urgency as he summarizes the armor of God and ties it all together with prayer:

> Pray in the Spirit at all times and on every occasion. Stay alert and be persistent in your prayers for all believers everywhere. And pray for me, too. Ask God to give me the right words so I can boldly explain God's mysterious plan that the Good News is for Jews and Gentiles alike. I am in chains now, still preaching this message as God's ambassador. So pray that I will keep on speaking boldly for him, as I should.
>
> EPHESIANS 6:18-20

Read these verses closely, and you will see that Paul recognizes the spiritual battle. He connects these verses to the preceding passage about the armor of God, but his words also convey urgency. Paul knew that all believers are in a spiritual war—not with each other, but with "evil rulers and authorities of the unseen world" (Ephesians 6:12). For Paul, victory over these unseen forces could not happen without prayer—so he repeatedly calls for prayer in Ephesians 6.

Because the battle is ongoing, Paul tells us to "pray in the Spirit at *all times* and on *every occasion*" (Ephesians 6:18, italics added). Never is there a time in the battle when we do not need to pray in the power of the Spirit and according to the will of the Father— just as the Spirit does when he intercedes for us (Romans 8:26-27). The warfare will not stop, and neither should our praying. Indeed, if we are to be alert to the conflict, ever aware of what the enemy is doing to hinder the work of God around us, we must pray consistently and persistently.

Just as Jesus taught his disciples in Luke 18, the believers in Ephesus were also called to be persistent in prayer even when they might have wanted to give up in the conflict. And did you notice the focus of their prayers? They were to pray *for all believers everywhere*. That sounds like a massive prayer list, but that is exactly the point: Every believer needs prayer because every believer is in the battle, whether he or she realizes it or not.

At *all* times. On *every* occasion. With *all* perseverance. For *all* believers *everywhere*. That is how we are to pray in the spiritual battle.

Now compare Paul's expectations to the way many of us pray for others today. Most of the time, we pray for others only when we hear they have a need (again praying reactively rather than proactively). The rest of the time, we leave each other uncovered in prayer while the enemy seeks to chew up every one of us.

I realize we cannot pray for every single believer in the world by name on a regular basis, but surely we can pray more often for those we know around us. We must pray for them not only when they are struggling in the battle, but also when they are living in victory; in that case, our prayer is for them to remain victorious even as the enemy comes after them.

Paul: "And pray for me, too."

The last time you asked someone to pray, what was your request? For your healing? For healing of a loved one? For a nonbelieving family member to be saved? For financial help? For wisdom? For strength in tough times? For guidance? As I think about this question, my most recent requests were for God to grant me wisdom in writing, give me stamina in weariness, and save a friend and a loved one who continue to reject the gospel. All these prayer requests I have mentioned are valid ones, but they are quite different from what Paul asked for himself in Ephesians 6.

What was Paul's request? For boldness to preach the gospel.

What catches my attention is Paul's location when he makes this request. He is in prison precisely for preaching the gospel boldly! Some believers might question why God did not protect Paul from arrest, and when he was imprisoned, it might have appeared as if the enemy had the upper hand. But that wasn't the case. Prison walls had not stopped Paul from preaching before, and he had no intention of stopping now. What he knew, however, was that he needed the prayers of God's people in order to remain steadfast. Persistent prayer by God's people on Paul's behalf would lead to his persistence in preaching, no matter the cost.

You might remember how the church responded similarly in Acts 4 when Peter and John were told by the authorities never again to speak or teach in the name of Jesus. The Jewish leaders threatened them and then released them—but only because all the people were glorifying God for healing a lame man. And rather than stop preaching, the church prayed for "great boldness" (Acts 4:29). As a result of this prayer, the building where they were meeting shook, and the disciples "preached the word of God with boldness" (Acts 4:31). Praying for boldness in preaching the gospel is always a good prayer.

Paul also asked the believers in Colossae to pray that he would speak the gospel clearly as God opened hearts to listen to him (Colossians 4:2-4). In that same letter, he reminds believers that Jesus created all the powers, including those that eventually rebelled against God (Colossians 1:15-16). He cautioned them against believing false teachings that come from "the spiritual powers of this world" (Colossians 2:8, 20). Thus, spiritual warfare was evident in Colossae, as it was in Ephesus. But the good news is that Jesus disarmed the powers of darkness through his death on the cross (Colossians 2:15). That is a message worth proclaiming clearly! The enemy surely wanted to hinder the message that Paul proclaimed, so Paul proactively asked for prayer support from the believers in these early churches. We would be wise to follow his example.[8]

Personal Reflection: Who is praying for you to proclaim the gospel boldly and clearly? If no one, who is the person you might ask to intercede for you in this way?

We learn from these Bible passages that victory in spiritual warfare does not always mean escaping the immediate conflict; instead, it is staying faithful to the task despite the battle. It is refusing to surrender to the enemy's arrows when the greater call of faithfulness to God rings in our ears. Paul committed himself to that kind of faithfulness, but he knew he needed prayer support to live out that goal. Knowing that Paul ran his race faithfully to the end (2 Timothy 4:7), we can assume the believers continually prayed for him to be obedient in sharing the good news.

The Evangelistic Focus of Prayer in the Battle

Listen to a person's prayer requests, and you can learn much about him or her. Just like the Pharisee and the tax collector in

Luke 18:9-14 reveal their hearts by their prayers in Jesus' parable, we reveal our burdens and priorities by our prayers and our prayer requests. In my years of pastoral ministry, I quickly learned who would pray about missions, neighbors, finances, politics, and even about their favorite sports teams. Paul's burden was clearly connected to sharing the gospel.

Why did Paul so strongly ask the believers to pray for his evangelistic efforts? The answer lies in how he understood the spiritual condition of nonbelievers. In several of his portrayals of the lost, Paul describes them in terms of spiritual conflict:

> If the Good News we preach is hidden behind a veil, it is hidden only from people who are perishing. Satan, who is the god of this world, has blinded the minds of those who don't believe. They are unable to see the glorious light of the Good News. They don't understand this message about the glory of Christ, who is the exact likeness of God.
>
> 2 CORINTHIANS 4:3-4

> Once you were dead because of your disobedience and your many sins. You used to live in sin, just like the rest of the world, obeying the devil—the commander of the powers in the unseen world. He is the spirit at work in the hearts of those who refuse to obey God.
>
> EPHESIANS 2:1-2

> He has rescued us from the kingdom of darkness and transferred us into the Kingdom of his dear Son, who purchased our freedom and forgave our sins.
>
> COLOSSIANS 1:13-14

Gently instruct those who oppose the truth. Perhaps God
will change those people's hearts, and they will learn the
truth. Then they will come to their senses and escape
from the devil's trap. For they have been held captive by
him to do whatever he wants.

2 TIMOTHY 2:25-26

The descriptions are vivid and painful at the same time.
Nonbelievers follow the devil. Satan has blinded them to the truth
of the gospel. They live in darkness. The enemy holds them in his
trap. They are dead in their disobedience, and the devil wants to
hold them in his grasp. He does not give them up easily.

God's plan, on the other hand, is for believers to share the
gospel so that the lost might believe and find freedom in Christ.
Look at how Jesus defined Paul's call to ministry:

I am sending you to the Gentiles to open their eyes, so
they may turn from darkness to light and from the power
of Satan to God. Then they will receive forgiveness for
their sins and be given a place among God's people, who
are set apart by faith in me.

ACTS 26:17-18

The Gentiles were blinded and living in darkness under the
power of the enemy, but God was sending Paul their way.

Through Paul's preaching and the work of the Holy Spirit,
everything would change for nonbelievers who trusted Christ.
Formerly blinded, now they would see. Living at one point in
darkness, now they would live in the light. Guilty as sinners, now
they would find forgiveness. Freed from the power of the enemy,
now they would live in the joy of being part of God's family. Satan

would not win in their lives. No wonder Paul wanted prayer support to proclaim the gospel boldly and clearly! The life-giving message is too great to settle for anything less.

As I write these words, my mind is drawn to missionaries I know who are living on the front lines of the spiritual battle around the world. One serves in a war-torn country where peace seems but a distant dream. Another friend and his family live in an area where persecution is aimed at any faith other than the prevailing one. Another friend was kicked out of one country for sharing his faith, but simply moved to another place where the gospel had not yet been preached. A retired missionary I know is a hero to generations of other missionaries for his faithfulness during a time of great upheaval and danger in the country where he served. All these missionaries will tell you the same thing: The prayers of God's people are critical to their staying faithful in the midst of seemingly nonstop spiritual warfare. They continue to proclaim the Good News in dangerous places because they know God's people stand behind them.

How about you? Are you praying for missionaries around the world to share the gospel? For your pastor? For your small group leader? For your spouse and your children? For yourself? I can only imagine what the church could accomplish if we prayed for each other to be bold and clear in evangelism. The enemy's grip on people loosens under the power of prayer.

Making It Personal

To pursue or continue in spiritual victory, review and apply the personal applications discussed in this chapter. First, make sure you are wearing the full armor of God (Ephesians 6:10-17). Paul rightly charged the Ephesians to be fully armed as they prayed for him, and it is good for us to remember that admonition. Review the descriptions of God's armor earlier in the chapter, and ask God to show you where you need to grow. Remember, we must wear *all* the armor in this battle.

Second, ask someone to help you strengthen any weak areas in your armor. We can make a commitment to grow, but we typically do not disciple ourselves well. By God's design, we need others to walk alongside us. Be honest with a trusted friend or family member about the areas where you need to grow—both for your sake and for the sake of the church. Your prayers will be more powerful, and your church will become more prayerful, if everyone wears the full armor of God as they pray.

Third, choose to partner with another believer to pray for each other's evangelistic efforts. Pray for boldness, clarity, and open doors to share the gospel. Then hold each other accountable to share the gospel with others. Praying together is a great starting point, but prayer alone is insufficient if we are unwilling to tell others about Jesus.

Finally, talk to your church's leaders, a missions agency, or some missionaries themselves about ways you and your church can support evangelistic efforts around the world through prayer. Cross-cultural workers face unique challenges every day. They are often isolated from other believers. Loneliness is not uncommon. Just knowing that someone is praying for them is a tremendous encouragement as they engage people caught in the devil's snare.

Praying for Victory

I'll give away my age here, but I still have a daily newspaper delivered to my home (and probably will for as long as that is an option). I use the paper as a prayer list of sorts—praying through stories I read about the needs and issues in our country and around the globe.

Recently, I have been struck by the number of stories about ongoing political and military conflicts. Some have been going on for decades, if not longer. In some cases, the local history is one of back-and-forth battles, with each side winning its share but no one achieving final victory. I hope these conflicts will soon come to an end, but history makes me wonder. As long as there are people involved, there is bound to be conflict. We don't know when these battles will end, nor do we know who will win.

Not so with the spiritual conflict in the heavens. Though battles continue to be fought, we know that Christ is already the winner. God alone knows when he will vanquish the enemy forever, but we know for certain that Satan's days are numbered. In the meantime, we join this spiritual battle clad in the armor of God and warring through prayer. In God's unique plan, we engage from a posture of humility and need. As we submit to God in prayer and obedience, the devil will flee.

Praying Leaders

I AM FIVE FEET eight inches tall, and I think I am shrinking as I age. But there was a time as a young teenager when I was one of the taller players on my baseball team. Everyone else kept on growing after I stopped, but in those days most of them looked up to me (literally). Because I was taller than the others, I played first base, which meant I was involved in many of the plays when my team was in the field.

I was also older than most of the other players, so my coach called on me to be a leader on the team. Many decades later, I can still remember some of the things he challenged me to do.

- Keep the team pumped up, even when we were losing.

- Start the chatter to disrupt the focus of the opposing batters.

- Remind the other infielders how many outs there were.

- Call out who should catch an infield pop-up if two players had a chance.

- Serve as the cutoff man on throws from the outfield.

"Chuck," the coach told me, "I need you to be an example, a positive leader for the rest of this team." The fact that the coach trusted me with that responsibility was a huge boost to my confidence. He gave me greater purpose, and I know I became a better ballplayer and more focused as a person because he expected me to lead.

As I think about the power of a praying church, I cannot help but think about the role of leadership. When it comes to infusing prayer into the DNA of a church, most leaders need someone to challenge them in that regard. Leaders need to be reminded—and challenged—to model prayer in their own lives, to encourage others to pray, and to live by faith even when it might seem as if the enemy is winning. Church leaders are to be "player-coaches" in prayer—praying on the front lines of ministry themselves while also coaching and encouraging other believers to pray.

If you are a leader in your church, in whatever capacity, this chapter is for you. Whether prayer will become part of the DNA of your church depends largely on you and others leading from your knees.

Why Leaders Matter in Prayer

To be honest, some of the most prayerful people I know are not pastors, and they are not always recognized as church leaders. Many of these prayer warriors are behind the scenes, almost hidden. And though they pray with passion and persistence, the congregation hasn't caught the same passion. Often that's because the leaders of the church don't share that passion either. If that statement describes you as a leader, here are some reasons your influence matters if you want prayer to become part of your church's DNA.

Praying leaders are best at casting a vision for prayer.

The leader may be a pastor, a deacon, a small group leader, a ministry director, or any other leader in the congregation, but the core truth remains the same: We will be much more effective at casting a vision for prayer if we ourselves are praying with passion and persistence. Those we guide will be much more likely to follow our lead if they see not only our vision, but also our zeal for God and our desire to talk with him. They will want what we have. On the other hand, attempting to cast a vision for prayer will come across as weak and disingenuous if we aren't spending much time in prayer ourselves.

Leaders who pray can—and will—call others to pray with integrity.

We who strive to preach or teach the Bible inevitably encounter topics and issues that make us uncomfortable because our lives don't match up with our teaching. It is too easy in those situations to ignore the topic completely or give it less attention than the Bible warrants. Prayer is one of those topics. Pastors and teachers who don't pray much themselves are not likely to give significant attention to the discipline of prayer in their teaching.

On the other hand, leaders who pray well will not hesitate to call others to prayer. Because they practice what they preach, no one can accuse them of hypocrisy. They look forward to teaching texts that deal with prayer. They love telling stories of answered prayer in their lives. They enjoy writing blogs and articles about the topic, and they have no problem promoting prayer meetings and conferences. They also delight when church members ask them to pray because the members know they really do pray.

Leaders who pray often model and teach prayer by their own heartfelt, humble public prayers.

Not all prayer warriors will pray publicly without hesitation, but many I know do. Those in positions of leadership will likely have greater opportunities to pray. Those who pray consistently in private will find public prayer that much easier. They love to talk to God, and the setting almost doesn't matter.

When they pray aloud, people listen. A sense of holiness and intimacy hangs in the air. Like eavesdroppers on a cherished spiritual moment between God and one of his children, we listen and learn. Here is how scholar D. A. Carson summarizes it: "Public praying is . . . an opportunity to instruct or encourage or edify all who hear the prayer."[1]

I am reminded of Brother Jack, one of my pastoral heroes. He often challenged me to have a "sweetheart love" for Jesus—that is, a love that is fascinated with Jesus, loves to be with him, and strives to please him. This kind of love means you cannot wait to "pick up the phone" and call Jesus—just like many of us called our fiancées multiple times a day when we were dating. It means you sacrifice much to be with Christ in prayer.

When Brother Jack prayed, you could hear his sweetheart love for Jesus in his voice. He talked to Jesus with no pretense, no seminary language, no concern that others were listening. The prayer was one needy friend talking to the only friend who could meet those needs. I wanted to pray like Brother Jack did, and I listened intently whenever he spoke to our heavenly Father.

Praying leaders show the work of God in their lives as he conforms them to his image.
We have already looked at Jesus' prayer life, but remember he prayed in such a way that others wanted him to teach them how to pray. He taught his disciples about prayer, and he took them away from the crowds to pray. More specifically, he prayed that the Father would make his disciples holy even as he protected them from the enemy. Jesus, our role model for leading others, led from his knees—and we imitate him when we do the same as God conforms us to his image. Thus, our commitment to prayer is evidence that we are growing in the right direction under God's grace.

Personal Reflection: Which of the reasons that leaders matter in prayer most grabs your attention? Why?

Biblical Examples of Leaders Who Prayed
One of the first books I ever read on leadership was J. Oswald Sanders's *Spiritual Leadership*. I still have my original copy, marked up by a desperate young pastor seeking guidance. The pages are now yellowed with age, but I can still see these faint highlights I marked years ago:

> The spiritual leader should outpace the rest of the church, above all, in prayer.

> The goal of prayer is the ear of God. Prayer moves others through God's influence on them. It is not our prayer that moves people, but the God to whom we pray.

> Great leaders of the Bible were great at prayer.[2]

Looking back, I now realize that the burden I felt to pray as I read this classic did not automatically result in my praying more. It did, however, cause me to see more clearly the examples of praying leaders in the Bible, and it helped me pay more attention to praying leaders around me. I have learned through these studies that leaders carry many burdens that necessitate prayer. Perhaps one of these sample stories from the Scriptures will encourage you to pray more as you carry the burdens of ministry.

Moses: Praying for God's grace on a rebellious people

Pastoral ministry sometimes frustrates me, especially when church members don't reflect the character of Christ in their actions. After reading about what Moses faced with the people of God, however, I complain less often. I cannot imagine what it was like to lead a people who continually questioned, complained, rebelled, and even turned to other gods. Had I been their leader, I might have been tempted to pray for God to bring down his wrath on them— but that is not what Moses did.

In Exodus 32:11-14, Moses prays that God would relent in his anger toward his people after they created their own false god while Moses was up on Mount Sinai. God even offered to consume the rebellious people and make a great nation of Moses, but that is not what Moses wanted. He prayed that God would honor his own name by keeping his covenant with Abraham and thus show to other nations his power and grace. God heard Moses' prayers and did not destroy his people.

Then, when God determined he would send only an angel to lead his stiff-necked people on their journey (rather than risk destroying them by his own presence), Moses again stepped in through prayer. He wanted God himself—not an angel—to lead them, and his prayer was clear: "If you don't personally go with us, don't make us leave this place. How will anyone know that you look favorably on me—on me and on your people—if you don't go with us? For your presence among us sets your people and me apart from all other people on the earth" (Exodus 33:15-16). So important was God's presence to Moses that he did not want his people to take another step if God was not with them. He had no intention of leading them forward if he were doing so on his own.

Church leadership is fraught with this kind of tension. No one wants to lead without God's leading, though I fear we often do. We press on in our church activities, ever mindful of the latest ideas for growth, and turn to God only when our own efforts fail. To say, "Lord, we are not going to take another step unless we know you are leading us" makes sense spiritually, but it slows down the process practically. So, instead, we lead first and pray second—and that is backward leadership. Unfortunately, that may especially be true when we are trying to deal quickly with a rebellious, toxic congregation.

If that description characterizes your church, know that I have been praying proactively for any reader who faces that scenario. You are not alone in whatever battle you face. And I encourage you to seek God's wisdom, will, and direction before you determine the best way to lead your congregation. God's honor is at stake, and you should desire for him to work in your rebellious congregation in such a way that his name is glorified. Ask him to give you glimpses of his glory—and trust him to hear you. Praying and giving him your burden will strengthen you and give you peace.

Joshua: Praying for clarity for a defeated people

Sometimes leaders pray for others with intentionality and direction because they know exactly what they are facing. Moses' prayer is an example of that kind of prayer. He knew what the people had done and prayed accordingly. In other cases, leaders don't know what's happening—both positively and negatively—behind the scenes. Sometimes the best thing we can do is pray for insight.

Joshua's leadership of God's people into battle at the city of Ai is an example of this latter scenario.³ The Israelites had been uniquely victorious in defeating the city of Jericho through a strange battle plan involving armies marching and walls collapsing (Joshua 6). When they prepared to attack Ai, however, they were certain they could win with less effort. After all, the armies of Ai were few, and large numbers of warriors would not be necessary (Joshua 7:3). We have no record of whether they prayed before going into battle, but their failure to pray when dealing with the Gibeonites later in Joshua shows us they made other decisions without seeking the Lord's guidance (Joshua 9:14). Regardless, we know that the people of Ai defeated the Israelites in a rout.

Joshua, their leader, was overwhelmed and confused by this sound defeat. He and the elders grieved, mourned, and bowed to the ground in response to their loss. Joshua, not knowing why they had lost after their rousing victory at Jericho, rightly cried out to the Lord (Joshua 7:6-9). Like Moses before him, he prayed about God's name and reputation now that his people had been defeated. Knowing the Israelites were vulnerable, their enemies would attack them, overtake them, and dishonor God's name by defeating his people. Joshua could not fathom why God would let that happen.

What Joshua didn't know was that one of his people, Achan, had taken spoils from Jericho in direct contradiction to God's command (Joshua 7:1). Their defeat at Ai was the result of God's judgment on the nation for Achan's actions. Secret sin had led to a very public defeat.

When Joshua prayed for clarity, though, God did something unusual: He told him to stop praying, get off his face, and deal with the sin in the camp (Joshua 7:10-15). There is a time to pray, and there is a time to act on our prayers—and the time for action had come for Joshua. His time of prayer helped him receive clarity about what was secretly happening, but God gave him that clarity so he might respond appropriately.

It might be that your congregation seems to be continually in defeat. You are giving your best, and you have no ongoing sin issues in your own life as far as you know. Still, you know that something isn't right. You sense that the enemy is winning in your congregation. I have no way of knowing what might be going on, but I do know what the best Christian leaders do in situations like this: They pray, and then they act. They turn to the Father to determine what is going on behind the curtain. They prayerfully evaluate what might be happening, and they deal with whatever they find. They do not act without praying, nor do they pray without acting.

Jehoshaphat: Praying for the Lord's help when overwhelmed

Imagine this scene. You are the king, and three armies have joined forces against you. The combined armies are vast. Word has now come that the enemy is nearby, and you feel powerless. You may be the leader, but you are not sure what to do. So, what *do* you do?

King Jehoshaphat of Judah walked in these shoes. The armies of Moab and Ammon, along with some of the Meunites, had combined their forces to attack Israel, and the king was terrified. To his credit, he did what he needed to do: He "begged the LORD for guidance" and called the nation to fast (2 Chronicles 20:3). In their desperation, the people followed the king's lead and came to Jerusalem to seek the Lord.

Jehoshaphat's prayer in this difficult situation is one of my favorite prayers in the Bible. First, he praises God for who he is: "the God who is in heaven . . . ruler of all the kingdoms of the earth . . . powerful and mighty" (2 Chronicles 20:6). Next, he confesses their desperate need for God. They feel powerless against the invading armies, and they don't know what to do. It was what they *did*, however, that is most inspiring to me: They looked to the Lord for his help. As several English translations of the Bible put it, "We do not know what to do, but our eyes are on you" (2 Chronicles 20:12, NIV, ESV, NRSV).

That is what prayer does: It locks our eyes on God. As you serve as a leader in your church, I am sure you face situations where the forces of Satan have rallied against you. You will confront situations in which you simply have no idea what to do, and you may feel powerless against the world's influence. When those times come, recognize your responsibility to call your church members to prayer.

Pray. Fast. Seek God. Trust. Lead the way. God is not overwhelmed by what overwhelms you and your congregation. And if by chance you question that assertion, read the rest of the story of Jehoshaphat in 2 Chronicles 20. God answers the king's prayer by raising up a prophet, giving them another strange battle plan (they were not to fight at all), and turning the invading armies against each other. Israel's enemies actually destroyed each other while God's people sang his praises! God's answers to our prayers may surprise us, but we can trust him when we seek him.

Paul: Praying regularly for God's church

Paul loved the churches he influenced, and that love is evident in the way he prayed for those congregations. He thanked God for them (Romans 1:8-10; 1 Corinthians 1:4), prayed they would be filled with knowledge, hope, and peace (Ephesians 1:18; Colossians 1:9; 2 Thessalonians 3:16), and asked the Father to grow their love for each other (Philippians 1:9).

Moreover, Paul prayed on an ongoing basis for these believers. We noted a few of these passages in a previous chapter, but read again the words he used to describe his commitment:

Day and night I bring you and your needs in prayer to God.
ROMANS 1:9

I always thank my God for you and for the gracious gifts he has given you.
I CORINTHIANS 1:4

I have not stopped thanking God for you. I pray for you constantly.
EPHESIANS 1:16

We have not stopped praying for you since we first heard about you.
COLOSSIANS 1:9

We always thank God for all of you and pray for you constantly.
I THESSALONIANS 1:2

We never stop thanking God.
I THESSALONIANS 2:13

Night and day we pray earnestly for you.
I THESSALONIANS 3:10

We keep on praying for you.
2 THESSALONIANS 1:11

Night and day I constantly remember you in my prayers.

2 TIMOTHY 1:3

Why was Paul so committed to pray for the churches he loved and the young men he mentored? In part, he recognized God's work in the lives of these people, and he was dedicated to thanking and praising God for it. Through his prayers, he sought to encourage the believers to remain faithful. He also was fully aware of the spiritual battle and the importance of praying for one another (Ephesians 6:18-20). As a good leader burdened for others to follow the Lord, he did what he expected others to do; in fact, Paul's "whole ministry was grounded in, and developed from, prayer."[4]

I can only wonder how the churches I pastored would have been different had I prayed for them like Paul prayed for people in his day. I prayed, but seldom with Paul's passion and focus. I certainly did not pray so regularly that I could use descriptors such as *night and day*, *always*, or *constantly*. I'm certain I didn't always pray sufficiently when church members faced attacks from the enemy. Looking back, I have to admit I did not always love my church as I should have. Had I loved them more, I would have prayed for them more. If that is your story as well, I hope this book encourages you to pray more often and more boldly.

Personal Reflection: How regularly do you pray for those you lead? How might you improve your efforts?

Needed: Praying Pastors

One of the most life-changing books I've ever read is E. M. Bounds's *Pastor and Prayer*. As a pastor myself, I cringe in conviction when I read these words:

> Where are the Christlike leaders who can teach the
> modern saints how to pray and set them to do it? Do
> we realize we are raising up a prayerless set of saints? . . .
> No one but praying leaders can have praying followers.
> Praying apostles will beget praying saints. A praying
> pulpit will beget praying pews.[5]

Of course, the opposite may be true as well. A non-praying pulpit will produce non-praying pews.

For several decades now, I have been privileged to study churches as a pastor, professor, and church consultant. Over the years, I have met many loving and devoted pastors. At the same time, I have recognized two areas where the pastor's influence—or lack thereof—is especially important.

First, I have never seen a church deeply committed to the great commission without a pastor whose heart beats for evangelism and missions. My friend Al Jackson, for example, spent more than four decades pastoring Lakeview Baptist Church in Auburn, Alabama. I never traveled with Brother Al on his many missions trips around the world—particularly in Africa—but I was blessed to help with his church-based intern program that required two summers of North American and international missions work. That component of the program certainly came from the passion of the pastor.

I have been with Brother Al as he did evangelism on the campus of Auburn University. He always led the way in evangelizing that campus. His testimonies of changed lives were both past and present tense, and you could tell he believed God would use him again to change lives. Given his leadership, I am not surprised that Lakeview has the great commission reputation it has.

Second, I have never seen a strongly praying church without a strongly praying pastor. Some congregations may have pockets of prayer here and there, but I have never seen DNA-level prayer in a church without a praying pastor. Again, Al Jackson is a great role model (and it's often the case that great commission pastors are also praying pastors). I have been in Al's "prayer closet" in his office, with pictures of missionaries for whom he prays covering the walls. Moreover, Lakeview Church is so committed to prayer that they have a full-time minister of missions and prayer.

I wish I could say all pastors pray like Brother Al does. My evidence is anecdotal, but many pastors who are honest with me talk about their struggles with establishing a consistent prayer life. I have thought much about these discussions in light of my own ongoing desire to continue growing in prayer, and I have reached some uncomfortable conclusions about the reasons behind our struggle.

1. In many cases, church leaders themselves were raised in churches that did not teach them how to pray. It is especially problematic when the pastors are among the untrained ones. Learning to pray on the fly is not the best way to learn, but it is how many of us have done it.

2. Prayer is often not a primary focus of our theological training. My own seminary education required *no* classes that helped me learn how to pray. Teaching prayer is seen as the responsibility of the local church, not the seminary. I agree that the local church should be the primary place of discipleship, but our seminaries have a responsibility to prepare our pastors in this regard. More seminaries have begun correcting this problem, though not sufficiently yet, in my opinion. A single class that addresses prayer is only a start.

3. Many pastors are such hands-on *doers* that taking time to shut ourselves away to pray may seem like not the best use

of our time. There is always another sermon to prepare, a meeting to lead, a family to visit, training to schedule, staff evaluations to conduct, or perhaps a carpet to vacuum or baptistry to fill. Who has time to devote even thirty minutes a day to prayer?

4. Often, pastors are hesitant to tell anyone that they struggle with prayer. After all, they are supposed to be a spiritual leader and role model—the one to whom the congregation looks as an example of how to live a victorious Christian life. Nobody wants to let people down, so pastors don't talk much about their prayer struggles. But if we pastors think it's better to struggle and remain silent than to admit our weakness and risk embarrassment, what are we really modeling for our churches? One of my hopes is that more pastors will come to realize that the pathway to growth in prayer sometimes begins with honest confession.

5. Maybe our greatest struggle with becoming praying pastors is that we can do a lot of ministry without much prayer, and our churches won't know the difference. Congregants may also struggle with prayer and have no idea what a genuine prayer life looks like. They may know their own deficiencies but not recognize the pastor's. Meanwhile, we fill the void with busyness and hope the "results" we produce will make up for weakness in prayer.[6]

Jim Cymbala, well-known pastor of the Brooklyn Tabernacle, describes this problem in terms of spiritual warfare: "Satan's main strategy with God's people has always been to whisper, 'Don't call, don't ask, don't depend on God to do great things. You'll get along fine if you just rely on your own cleverness and energy.'"[7] I know this whisper because regrettably I have listened to it in the past.

Making It Personal

Maybe you're a pastor who is hearing that same whispering voice of the enemy today. If so, I want to give you some practical suggestions—and some hope and encouragement.

1. **Gladly accept your responsibility as your church's chief prayer warrior.** Our responsibility as pastors is "to equip God's people to do his work" (Ephesians 4:12). Among other things, that calling requires us to pray and to model prayer for our congregations. When Peter Wagner was a professor at Fuller Seminary, he wrote this about his own studies of praying churches: "The prayer ministry of the local church will rise or fall on the leadership role of the pastor. . . . This does not mean they themselves do all the prayer ministry. Far from it. But they do hold themselves responsible and accountable for the quantity and quality of prayer in their church."[8]

   Just as Jesus and Paul led the way in teaching their disciples to pray, so must we, as pastors and teachers, lead the way in our churches. Moreover, we must do it with joy and conviction—not in a forced way based on our position of leadership. If we are not fully on board, our congregations will know. Our churches will not become praying churches if the people do not see a passion for prayer in us. So gladly accept your responsibility and prayerfully seek God's help.

2. **Be honest with others if prayer is a struggle for you.** Several years ago, I was living through a particularly dry

season of prayer. Talking to God was difficult, and when I did pray, I battled unbelief. I debated reading some books about prayer to see if they would help. One of those books was *A Passion for Prayer*, written by my pastoral mentor, Tom Elliff.[9]

As I picked up Tom's book, I approached it with two almost contradictory thoughts in mind. First, I wanted to hear from him because I knew his words would drip with integrity. Second, I did not want to hear from him because I knew I would never make it to where he was in his prayer journey. I feared I would experience embarrassment more than encouragement, conviction more than comfort, defeat rather than desire.

Still, I picked up the book. Imagine my relief when I read Tom's words in the first chapter:

> Several years ago I began to study the lives of great people of prayer. I could not escape the fact that God used men and women who were dedicated to the practice of prayer to change the course of history. The more I read, the more convicted I became of my own prayer-lessness. I had seen a certain measure of success in the pastorate and was considered by some to have arrived at a most enviable position. But now I found myself, without benefit of either human criticism or encouragement, under the searching eye of God. Alone before Him, I could not defend my utter lack of prayer.
>
> It was not that I did not *appear* to be a man of prayer. . . . But in reality, my personal prayer

altar was in ruins. Except for spasmodic peri-
ods of renewed effort, I just did not pray.[10]

Here was my hero admitting to anyone who read his
book that he had struggled with prayer. His honesty and
openness gave me courage to talk about my own battles
and begin on a journey toward growth.

You can strengthen your prayer life *today* by telling
somebody about your battle and asking him or her to pray
with you. Pray together each day in person or by phone
until prayer becomes a part of your daily practice. I suspect you will find other pastors who will not only be willing to pray with you, but who also need someone to help
them become better at prayer. Be bold enough to start that
conversation.

3. **Pray with and for your spouse.** If you are not already doing
   this, start praying with your spouse each day. Even if you
   spend only a few minutes praying together, a few minutes
   daily is better than none.

   Try this method as a starting point: Each day before you
   or your spouse leaves for work, take time to give the day to
   the Lord and ask for his guidance and blessing. Some morn-
   ings, I take my wife's hand and pray before I head to the gym
   at 5:00 a.m. I don't know if she is fully alert at that time, but
   I have learned how much she appreciates the prayer. Your
   day—and your marriage—will be better if you prioritize
   seeking the Lord with your spouse each day.

   As you pray *with* your spouse, you will naturally pray
   for your spouse, but I encourage you to also set aside time
   during the week to pray specifically for your spouse. Maybe

one of these ways I pray for my wife, Pam, will give you some direction:

a. **That she would simply walk with the Lord and live out his love.** Pam is the kindest, godliest person I have ever met, and my role is to prayerfully encourage her to continue in that way.

b. **That God would provide opportunities and wisdom for her to reach the lost and invest in younger women.** Pam is not a Bible scholar or trained counselor, but she studies God's Word, listens to others for wisdom, and trusts the Holy Spirit.

c. **That she would be comfortable in who she is as a professor/pastor's wife.** She is comfortable in her role, so this is not a prayer to change her. It is a prayer to encourage her.

d. **That she would never hesitate to speak truth to me.** She has always been willing to speak up when there is something I need to hear, and I want her to know I always welcome her thoughts.

e. **That God would maximize her gifts—and that I would be fully supportive.** I added the last part because Pam is an extreme extrovert with the gift of hospitality, and I am an extreme introvert who doesn't always feel like entertaining. Still, I love seeing Pam's joy when she serves others, and I want to support and encourage her gifts.

f. **That God would keep her healthy.** I confess that the COVID-19 crisis led me to pray much more in this direction.

g. **That she would know how grateful I am for her.** I cannot imagine life or ministry without her.

h. **That she would always have laughter in her life.** Her sense of humor caught my attention when I first met her, and I never want her to lose her laughter.[11]

4. **Give deliberate attention to the pastoral prayer during the Sunday morning service.** My point here assumes your church has a pastoral prayer in the order of service. If you do, I encourage you to prepare that prayer like you prepare your sermon each week. I am not opposed to spontaneity in praying, but neither am I opposed to writing a prayer ahead of time. Nothing about writing a prayer weakens its power or diminishes your role as a prayer leader. In fact, a well-constructed prayer that reflects your heart is better than a spontaneous prayer that seems obligatory or lacks focus.

Ronnie Floyd, a longtime pastor who has written much about prayer and fasting, also issued a call for returning the pastoral prayer to worship services.[12] During that time, pastors "stand in the gap" for the church, praying with conviction, passion, and authenticity. The time allotted for the prayer—four to five minutes, Floyd suggests—emphasizes the priority of prayer and requires the pastor to give significant time to preparing the prayer. Frankly, a congregation will tune out a five-minute spontaneous prayer that is unfocused and rambling—so get ready ahead of time. Your preparation in prayer will reap God's reward and bless his people.

If your order of service does not include a pastoral prayer, think about revising the service to make room for this significant time. Your church needs to hear you pray, and you need to teach them about prayer by the way you pray. At the appropriate time in the service, lead them to the throne of God through prayer. Invite them to participate as you talk to the Father on their behalf. Make sure they hear more about God than about you in your prayer; show them that the goal of prayer is to meet with God rather than to get something from him. Let them hear your love for God and for them. You will lead this time best if you have already prayerfully considered your words.

5. **Enlist a prayer leader and a prayer team to help you cast a vision for prayer.** The strongest praying churches I know have a praying pastor and a specific pastoral or lay leader (sometimes with a title such as "minister of prayer" or "director of prayer ministries") guiding the church's prayer efforts. The pastor casts the vision and models prayer, and the prayer leader oversees implementation of the vision. I affirm this approach, but I also see a place for establishing a churchwide prayer team.

   The role of the prayer team is to gather for prayer and to determine the best ways to build prayer into the DNA of the congregation. They work with the pastor and prayer leader to broaden the base of praying leaders in the church. They will also organize prayer trainings, connect with prayer leaders of each ministry, and coordinate various prayer efforts throughout the church. Ideally, the prayer team reflects the composition of the congregation, including older and younger members who can influence their own generations. This team is critical, so the pastor ought to be directly involved in enlisting the right members to join them. The size of the team will vary by church, but I suggest a team of no more than five members.

6. **Take advantage of "ten-minute segments" throughout the day. Use at least two or three segments each day to pray.** Sometimes we neglect to pray because we don't have an hour free to do it. But there's another way to capture an hour within your day—*in ten-minute segments*. No matter how busy we are, we all have brief breaks during the day when we can choose how to fill our time. If we're not careful, social media can gobble up those moments; but we can make the decision to use the time more wisely.

At least two or three times during the day, take ten minutes to pray.[13] Figure out in the morning when those times might be most available, and commit to using them for prayer. If you can find three times a day to pray, by the end of the day you will have prayed for half an hour—just not in consecutive minutes. *Start somewhere* and let the time grow.

You might use one ten-minute segment each day to pray through your church's membership roll, taking time to pray for active *and* inactive members. Take time to send a note that you prayed for them that day. Active members will appreciate the gift of your prayers, and inactive members just might renew their faith commitment after you have prayed for them. Our human efforts seldom succeed in reengaging inactive members, but interceding for them is hardly only a human effort.

Because praying with other believers matters, use at least two of your ten-minute segments each week to pray with someone else. The brevity of such prayers will not be burdensome for most church members, and many will be honored to pray with you. In fact, you can model prayer for these members as you pray about their needs.

7. **Enlist "Pastor's Prayer Partners."** I first heard about this concept at a John Maxwell conference I attended many years ago as a young pastor. When Maxwell spoke about dozens of prayer partners who prayed for him daily— including praying for him each Sunday prior to the service, I knew I needed folks to pray for me that way. My Pastor's Prayer Partners ministry never reached the level of John Maxwell's, but having church members pray for me each Sunday became an important part of my ministry. Even today, I meet with a small group who prays for me just prior to the Sunday morning service.

As a pastor myself, may I suggest some ways to pray for pastors?

a. **That we will walk in godliness.** Our ministry loses credibility if our walk doesn't match our words.

b. **That we will love our spouses like Christ loves the church.** We want our marriages to model for others the love of God.

c. **That we will be praying leaders.** That is the theme of this entire chapter.

d. **That we will proclaim the gospel boldly.** We need that kind of prayer support even more than Paul did.

e. **That we will finish well.** The enemy strikes at leaders, and nobody finishes well by accident. We need the prayers of God's people every day.

If you are a pastor who does not yet have partners praying for you, I encourage you to begin enlisting others who are willing to make this commitment on your behalf. Even just a few people praying regularly for you can make a difference. If you are a lay leader, ask your pastor how you might regularly partner with him in prayer. It might be that God will use you to start this kind of prayer ministry, and you can enlist other praying lay leaders.

Catching the Vision

Several years ago, I took a friend to a prayer conference where I was one of the speakers. He just wanted to hang out with me, but I wanted him to learn more about prayer. With excitement, I worked out a breakfast with several people on the morning of the conference so that my friend could meet the keynote speaker—an older man well known for his commitment to prayer.

At the breakfast, the speaker was unusually quiet, seemingly tired, and generally unengaging. To be honest, I feared that my friend would be bored by this man's presentation—and that I would too! I wasn't wrong . . . at least for the first part of his presentation.

When the speaker hit his stride talking about prayer and then led us in prayer, however, what had at first been a bit dry became a fire. He went on to speak and pray for more than an hour, and I don't think anyone was looking at the clock. As a holy prayer warrior was teaching us and modeling prayer for us, soaking it in was the only right thing to do.

If we're going to produce powerful churches with prayer in their DNA, this is the kind of leadership we need. May you and I strive to be that kind of person.

Getting Started: Praying Together

You MIGHT RECALL that one of my pastoral heroes is Charles Spurgeon, the famous nineteenth-century London-based preacher. Spurgeon was the pastor of the Metropolitan Tabernacle (formerly the New Park Street Chapel) from 1854 to 1892. From a membership of about 230 when Spurgeon arrived, the church saw more than 14,000 people join the church during his ministry.[1]

Every Monday night, church members joined together in a prayer meeting that became the underlying power source for this ministry. Listen to how Spurgeon describes it:

> The Prayer Meeting is an institution which ought to be very precious to us and to be cherished very much by us as a Church, for to it we owe everything. When our comparatively little Chapel was all but empty, was it not

a well-known fact that the Prayer Meeting was always full? And when the Church increased, and the place was scarcely large enough, it was the Prayer Meeting that did it all! When we went to Exeter Hall, we were a praying people, indeed. And when we entered on the larger speculation, as it seemed, of the Surrey Music-Hall, what cries and tears went up to Heaven for our success! And so it has been ever since. It is in the spirit of prayer that our strength lies! And if we lose this, the locks will be shorn from Samson and the Church of God will become weak as water. And though, we, as Samson did, go and try to shake ourselves as at other times, we shall hear the cry, "The Philistines are upon you," and our eyes will be put out, and our glory will depart unless we continue mighty and earnest in prayer.[2]

"If we lose this [spirit of prayer] . . . the Church of God will become weak as water," Spurgeon said. That sentence not only reflects the great preacher's heart, but it also helps us understand why so many North American churches are weak. They simply do not pray well, often because they are led by pastors who do not pray well. Thus, the focus of this chapter is to help you and your church think about ways to build prayer into your congregational DNA, and thereby strengthen your personal prayer life too.

Why Praying Together Matters

I have told some of my story in previous chapters. When I became a Christian at the age of thirteen, I began attending prayer meetings with other teenagers. At various times, we prayed for revival, for our church staff, and for our school administrators and teachers. No matter what else was going on in my life, I prioritized being there. Now, you might think I was going because of my commitment to prayer, but that wasn't it. I went because I wanted to be with my friends.

What I didn't know then, but have learned since, was the power of God's people praying together. Obviously, there is power in individual, private prayer—as Jesus showed us; but corporate prayer has a power of its own. It marked the early church, and we need it to mark our churches as well. Here are some reasons why gathering for prayer is so effective.

Praying together reflects the way God created us.

I mentioned earlier that my wife is an extrovert. She enjoys hosting people and being where the action is. I, on the other hand, am a strong introvert. I like to work by myself, I like time to think, and I like my private space. Don't get me wrong: I love my family, my church, and my sweet wife, and I enjoy interacting with other people one-on-one or in small group settings, but I am *energized* by solitude and quiet more than by hanging out with other people. At times I have even said to myself, "I have God in my life, and he's all I need. I don't really need other people to be happy." But then I read Genesis 2 again, and I'm reminded that "it is not good for the man to be alone" (Genesis 2:18).

It's important to note that Adam's need for someone else in his life was not the result of his falling into sin; it was by God's original design: "I will make a helper who is just right for him" (Genesis 2:18). God created us with a need not only for himself, but also for other people. He who is relational within himself as the Trinity made us relational beings as well.

I like the way one scholar describes this plan: "Isolation is not the divine norm for human beings; community is the creation of God."[3] In the relationships of community, we experience friendship, commitment, accountability, and support. We also express and share God's love as we serve each other. Praying together as brothers and sisters in Christ is one way we minister to one another in community.

Think about what happens when we humbly seek God together. Our personal agendas do not matter anymore. Egos disappear, at least temporarily. We open our hearts in vulnerability, and we share the weight of the burdens of others. More personally, your cries of anguish bring me to tears on your behalf. Our praying together says not only, "God, we need you," but also, "We need other believers." That is the way God created us.

The Bible speaks often of God's people praying together.

A quick look at the Old Testament shows God's people praying together, often during times of crisis. In one instance, after a great victory, the people sang God's praises for leading them across the Red Sea (Exodus 15:1-18). In the book of Judges, they repeatedly cry out to God when they find themselves oppressed by other nations (Judges 3:9, 15; 4:3; 6:6-10; 10:9-10, 15; 20:22-23, 26-28; 21:2-3). Their prayers may have been more an expression of pain than of repentance, but they nevertheless cried out to the Lord.

Ezra called the people to pray for God's protection as they returned to Jerusalem (Ezra 8:21-23). The Levites led the nation in a prayer of national confession in Nehemiah's day (Nehemiah 9:1-37). Likewise, the Psalms of Ascent (Psalms 120–134) were prayers to be sung together as the people made their way up to Jerusalem.

We know from our previous study that Jesus prayed with his disciples at times (e.g., the Mount of Transfiguration in Mark 9). But maybe the best way to see Jesus' commitment to corporate prayer is to review again the model prayer he taught his disciples (Matthew 6:9-13; Luke 11:2-4).[4] Sometimes we recite that prayer so automatically that we miss the fact that the pronouns throughout the prayer are plural: "*Our* Father," "give *us*," "forgive *us* . . . as *we* have forgiven those who sin against *us*," "don't let *us* yield to temptation," "rescue *us* from the evil one." The nature of this prayer reminds us that we are on this journey together as the people of God. In fact, praying together in community should be encouraging to us.

We also saw God's people praying together in our study of the prayer life of the early church. The book of Acts has multiple examples of believers praying together. From the followers of Christ praying before they replaced Judas in Acts 1 to Paul and his team praying for the disciples at Tyre in Acts 21, corporate prayer is the predominant type of prayer we see. Indeed, for the Christians in the early church, their task was so great that surely they knew they needed to support each other in prayer.

Praying together is an expression of our God-given unity.

It is almost impossible to read Jesus' prayer in John 17 and not see his requests that his followers be united:

> Now I am departing from the world; they are staying in
> this world, but I am coming to you. Holy Father, you have
> given me your name; now protect them by the power of
> your name so that they will be united just as we are.
> JOHN 17:11

> I am praying not only for these disciples but also for all
> who will ever believe in me through their message. I pray
> that they will all be one, just as you and I are one—as you
> are in me, Father, and I am in you. And may they be in
> us so that the world will believe you sent me. I have given

119

them the glory you gave me, so they may be one as we are one. I am in them and you are in me. May they experience such perfect unity that the world will know that you sent me and that you love them as much as you love me.

JOHN 17:20-23

When God adopts us as his children and places us in his family, he unites us to himself and to one another. He grants us such connection that calling each other *brother* and *sister* is more than just what we do when we cannot remember names; it is an expression of relationship that often goes deeper than our families of origin. By this unique unity, we show the world the transforming power of Christ. It is no wonder, then, that the enemy strives to create division among us—or that Jesus has already prayed for our unity in light of that battle. He wants us to be one like he and the Father are one.

There is indeed something powerful about the unity we express when we pray together. I think, for example, about community prayer events on the National Day of Prayer each year. I have participated in gatherings of believers from different denominations, different ethnicities, and different economic and educational levels. The gatherings have included pastors and laypeople, men and women, young and old. Sometimes the groups included folks whose native language was something other than English; yet, something happened when we all prayed together.

When we get on our knees together, prejudice loses its grip on us. Differences that need not divide us do not get in the way of our intercession. Our unity is built around a common Lord, a common gospel, and a common goal of reaching our community. Those same common factors unite us in our local churches as our congregations march forward together on our knees. Given the fractured nature of society today, the world needs to see that kind of gospel-centered unity. In unity, we fight *for* one another in prayer rather than *against* one another in conflict.

Praying together can teach us how to pray.

Most believers need help learning how to pray. We hear messages from the pulpit about prayer but still struggle. We see our church's prayer list, but the needs and names don't necessarily prompt us to pray. We might even read a book about prayer and still not pray more (though I hope that isn't the case for you as you're reading *this* book). Many Christians need all the help they can get to pray—and praying with other believers can help them move in the right direction.

First, simply meeting with others to pray can slow us down and encourage accountability in this discipline. Knowing that others expect us to join them in prayer adds weight to our commitment. The natural result is that we pray more, both individually and corporately. And even if our progress is slow, we are encouraged and accountable.

Second, others show us how to pray as they intercede for us when we cannot pray for ourselves. Maybe you have been in this kind of situation. You grieve some loss so deeply that words do not come. You are trying to pray for a wayward adult child, but it is difficult to keep trusting after years of prayer. Or maybe some unconfessed sin has made it impossible to pray, and simply being with other believers is both convicting and encouraging as they pray for your unspoken request. We hear them pray for us, and we learn how to pray for others.

Third, we learn about the burdens and needs of others as we pray together—and those burdens then become our own prayer burden. I have been in full-time ministry for more than forty years, and I recall many times when I first learned about a church member's need during a time of prayer with others. I usually wished that member would have told me as his pastor, but a posture of prayer removed any hurt or frustration. I simply joined the other believers in praying about those needs, both individually and corporately.

Praying together is one way we fight spiritual battles arm in arm.

A previous chapter helped us to see the reality of spiritual warfare. You might remember that the apostle Paul exhorted believers to "put on all of God's armor" (Ephesians 6:11) as we wrestle against powers in the unseen world. Like first-century warriors who walked forward in battle side by side with shields raised, we step onto the battlefield with other believers, united in prayer. We help each other put on the full armor of God so that we can stand *together* against the enemy.

I have been in prayer meetings where believers prayed for others who were losing the battle with discouragement, and the combined prayers of God's people brought encouragement. I have seen hope restored when believers prayed for God to break strongholds of sin; love renewed where demonic anger had reigned; and families repaired after the enemy had sought to tear them apart. And I have watched with other prayer warriors as God brought unity to congregations splintered under Satan's thumb.

Indeed, the power of praying together reminds us of the foolishness of trying to deal with spiritual conflict alone. Isolation can be a sign of egotism because it suggests we think we can handle a conflict by ourselves. It can be evidence of alienation—a problematic position from which to fight a supernatural enemy. New Testament scholar Clinton Arnold, an expert on the principalities and powers in Paul's writings, reminds us that the early church prayed together to arm one another for spiritual warfare. He calls this strategy "praying for the healthy" when believers pray for each other to resist temptation where they are most vulnerable to the enemy's arrows.[5]

Praying together matters. It reflects the Creation story, follows the Bible's pattern, shows our unity, teaches us to pray, and helps us win spiritual battles. You would think, then, that every church would be a praying congregation—but that isn't the case. For that reason, we need to talk about ways to evaluate a church's prayer DNA and build prayer into our own lives and into the life of our churches.

How Praying Together Becomes "Routine"

If every church understood the importance of praying together and genuinely made it their ongoing practice, I would feel no need to write this book. Some churches *do* pray together, but seldom with the zeal and tenacity of the early church or of Spurgeon's Metropolitan Tabernacle. Most churches, I fear, lose their passion for prayer somewhere along the way.

To understand how this happens, consider the life cycle of a church, as depicted by Robert Dale in his book *To Dream Again*.[6] Using Dale's diagram as a foundation, I want us to think about prayer at major points in the life of a church.

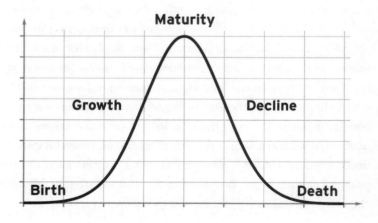

At the *birth stage*, most churches begin with an outward focus. They long for God to use them to reach their neighbors. They dream in visionary faith about how God might work through them. Just getting started, usually needing resources and desiring God's help, they pray. A lot. Together. Regularly. At the front end of their vision and desperate for God's glory to fall around them, they hit their knees.

At the *growth stage*, the church builds on their dreams by doing such things as setting goals, establishing polity, and putting structure in place. Prayer is still one of their commitments as they seek wisdom, but prioritizing prayer becomes more difficult amid growing numbers of events and activities. Nobody intentionally says, "We will pray less now," but a church calendar increasingly filled with activities typically leaves less room for members to pray together. The decline in prayer may be subtle but is nonetheless real.

The *maturity stage* is the pinnacle of the church's work, characterized by ongoing ministry. Busyness marks the church—and prayer too often becomes only one ministry option among others for members. The prayer warriors continue to pray, but they are outnumbered by those for whom prayer is not in their DNA. Most corporate prayer is now reactive rather than proactive, as we have seen in previous chapters. When "success" in ministry diminishes a church's sense of their dependence on God, the cry for prayer that motivated the church during the *birth stage* is no longer as strong.

If a church does not stay alert, it can begin to move in the wrong direction, into the *decline stage*. Growth becomes stagnant, perhaps because the congregation loses their outward focus or gets too comfortable where they are. The days of powerful growth are now past tense, and "I remember when" becomes a common phrase. Fractures begin to appear, and the church that does nothing will continue its decline toward the *death stage*.

We might hope that churches would begin to pray more as they start to slide down the wrong side of the bell curve, but my experience says that doesn't always happen. Sometimes the decline is so gradual that it goes unnoticed for some time. In other cases, the church in decline first retreats to familiar and comfortable ground, to protect what they have, before they genuinely seek God's guidance. By the time a church becomes polarized and divided, few members are calling for united prayer. Even churches that are striving for revitalization are susceptible to "fixing their problems" apart from seeking God in prayer for his direction and help. Only occasionally have I seen a church start the revitalization process with prayer, continue it with prayer, and rejoice in prayer when God finally turns things around.

What, then, is the answer? Again, Robert Dale's model is helpful. Though prayer is not his primary topic, his ideas for renewing churches in general can be applied to the goal of maintaining prayer as a priority. Church leaders must "dream again" as their church nears the top of the bell curve—before any decline sets in.[7] As the church reaches the *maturity stage*, they must renew their vision so they continually think outwardly—building off the dream, growing structures out of the dream, and extending the dream.[8]

The same is true for prayer in the church. The farther the local church travels down the wrong side of the bell curve, the less likely they will have the energy and focus for the work of renewal—even for prayer. The solution is for church leaders to call the congregation to prayer at the beginning of the growth curve and continue to take them there until prayer becomes an essential part of the church's DNA. Only by continuing to prioritize prayer will a church be able to stave off the slide into self-reliance and program-dependence. The vision to become a DNA-level praying church must continually be renewed and refreshed—the vision will stay alive because the church's leaders keep it alive and in front of the people.

The remainder of this chapter will help you move your congregation toward becoming a church with prayer in their DNA. These ideas are designed for corporate prayer, though some may apply just as easily to your personal prayer life.

Needed: Praying Lay Leaders

John was a lay leader in one of the churches I pastored. His role was chairman of the trustees, which meant he was responsible primarily for building and grounds. He and his team worked hard so our facilities reflected excellence for the glory of God. John was a quiet leader who listened more than he spoke and who spent significant time considering the most effective ways to do his job.

What I most remember about him, though, was that he prayed about every decision his team made—and he led his team to prioritize prayer in all they did. It might seem odd to think about praying about paint colors, lawnmower purchases, and contracted labor, but that was the way John operated. He sought God in all he did.

In that same church was Faye, who oversaw the women's missionary group. She loved missionaries, and her heart beat for the nations. She tried to make sure that the women's group—and by extension, the entire church—continually prayed for missions organizations, missionaries, national believers, and unreached people groups. So strongly did she believe in missions-focused prayer that she continually challenged me as pastor to keep that commitment in front of our congregation. She spoke to me respectfully and lovingly, but she usually let me know if we missed an opportunity to pray about the nations. In fact, I attribute much of my own commitment to missions today to Faye's influence on me years ago.

If a church wants to become a praying church, it will not happen without a praying pastor and praying lay leaders like John and Faye. Pastors cannot carry the responsibility alone. They may seek to invest in a few leaders, but no church will become a "house of prayer" (Luke 19:46) unless the lay leaders also support that goal. Prayer that stops at the pulpit misses the goal of growing a congregation with prayer in its DNA.

Why does it matter that lay leaders also lead the way in prayer? First, lay leaders are often more intimately connected with the congregation than the pastor is. They often know more about the needs of the congregation, and they can help keep the pastor informed about the flock.

Second, lay leaders often have more direct influence on members of the congregation. Especially as the church grows larger, the pastoral team must raise up other leaders to broaden the work base of the church and equip the next generation of leaders. Individual connections with the pastoral staff become more difficult to maintain as a church grows, so lay leaders become crucial members of the team. The pastor may teach and model prayer from the pulpit, but it is often the lay leaders, in team and mentoring relationships, who have more direct influence in modeling prayer for other members.

Third, lay leaders can be significant conduits *or* roadblocks to a praying church. On the one hand, leaders who pray well can equip others in their respective ministries to do the same. The prayer commitment of the pastor thus extends through the congregation. On the other hand, lay leaders can become an obstacle to reaching that goal if they are not praying leaders themselves. The vision may be clear from the pastor, but its implementation can be hindered at the lay leader level. Lay leaders uncommitted to prayer become a bottleneck in the church's efforts to develop a prayer DNA in the congregation.

So a praying church requires a praying pastor and praying lay leaders. It also requires intentionality, structure, and accountability. Though I want you to recognize the importance of thinking strategically about your church becoming a prayer-driven church, I don't want you to be overwhelmed by numerous ideas that may be difficult to implement. Instead, I offer you some simple, practical ways to put prayer into the DNA of your congregation.

Making It Personal

You probably already know some strategies for prayer, such as prayer lists, prayer chains, and the ACTS model (Adoration, Confession, Thanksgiving, Supplication). You and your church might have tried some methods that didn't work long-term. My goal here is not to introduce new, revolutionary ideas, but to challenge you to build prayer into what you are already doing. We do not need new methods; we simply need to prioritize prayer in all we do.

Prioritize prayer in your church's primary worship service.

Let me ask you a question. If I were to attend your church's worship service next Sunday, what would I know about your church after one service? That you have great music? That the pastor is a strong communicator? That your folks are friendly? That you strive for excellence? What conclusions would I reach based on one service?

I'm sure you can anticipate my next question: Would I conclude from your church's worship service that your church believes in and prioritizes prayer?

In almost every church I pastored, we prayed an invocation, an offertory prayer, and a benediction. I typically prayed after reading the Scripture passage for the morning message. The pattern was so routine that I doubt anyone gave it much thought. We prayed because it was the next item in the bulletin more than because we wanted to spend time with God. How about your church?

Here are some ways to prioritize prayer in the worship service. First—as I encouraged in chapter 5—include a prepared pastoral prayer in the order of service. If you are the pastor, assume this responsibility with seriousness and passion. Prepare the pastoral prayer as you prepare your sermon.

Second, establish a time to pray for a different ministry of the church each week. The prayer need not be long, but it should be focused and substantive. Plan well, and use this prayer time strategically to encourage your laborers. Imagine the joy that parents and children's workers may experience when prayer is offered specifically for the children's ministry. Or the excitement of the praise team or choir as you publicly cover their efforts in prayer. Personalized prayer for specific ministries can both encourage and motivate those who serve in those ministries—not to mention what God might choose to do in response to your prayers.

Third, use the entire worship service for prayer at least twice a year. Again, prayerfully plan well. Enlist people to pray particular prayers (for example, adoration, confession, thanksgiving, and supplication/intercession), and encourage them to write their prayers ahead of time. Plan worship songs related to prayer. Include times of silent prayer, and offer prompts as the congregation prays. Consider asking attenders to write prayer requests on cards and place them on the altar at some point during the service—and later ask the prayer team to pray about these requests. Stay focused on the goal throughout the service: praying as a congregation.

Do not be afraid to schedule regular church-wide prayer meetings.

That heading might seem odd, but here's my point: Because prayer meeting attendance has so clearly declined over the years, many churches have stopped having regular prayer meetings. If they meet for prayer, it's typically in response to a pressing need (praying reactively), rather than simply to spend time with God and with one another. Regularly scheduled prayer meetings seem to be a thing of the past, but they don't have to be. Churches with prayer in their DNA will gather regularly to pray as a congregation.

By planning well and giving direction to the prayer concerns, you can avoid the common traps of having your prayer meetings become gossip sessions cloaked in prayer or boring prayer times without intentionality. John Onwuchekwa, teaching pastor of Cornerstone Church in Atlanta, emphasizes the importance of prayer meetings at his church.[9] His congregation meets at least monthly for prayer, and they gather with clear intentionality.

For example, they prioritize the meeting by scheduling no other church activities during that time. They begin each prayer meeting with a brief (five- to fifteen-minute) "encouragement from God's Word" to guide the prayer that night, and they limit prayer requests to "kingdom concerns, whole body concerns, and major life concerns."[10] Small groups may pray about more personal, individual health needs and concerns, but the congregational prayer meeting focuses on the entire body. They call on members to pray during their prayer meetings, but they limit their time. With good planning, nobody monopolizes the praying.

As your church plans its prayer meetings, don't worry about the numbers. Some church members may never get on board. But remember: A prayer ministry with a few strong prayer warriors is better than vast numbers of people who really don't pray much. To have an effective prayer meeting, according to Onwuchekwa, all you need are "burdens, and brothers and sisters who are willing to pray."[11] Schedule prayer meetings and begin to move your church in the direction of being a praying church, even if only a few members join you at first.

Pray, and build prayer training into your church's membership class.

Some years ago, I wrote *Membership Matters*, a book based on a study of churches with membership classes. At the time, more churches were striving to raise the bar of membership, and I wanted to help them learn from others who were already capitalizing on a new member class. One of the goals was to determine what churches were teaching their prospective new members.

I recently returned to that study to see how many of the fifty-two respondents from various locations and denominations included training in spiritual disciplines in their membership classes. To my surprise, 51 percent of the churches taught something about spiritual disciplines, but that topic ranked far below fifteen *other* topics that were more common. (In case you're wondering, church doctrine, expectations for members, and the church's mission/vision topped the list).[12]

If your church has a membership class, I understand the scheduling difficulty of adding another topic to the class. Still, you can show new members the priority of prayer in the congregation by incorporating some or all of the following:

- Start the class with an intentional time of prayer for each of the new members and their families. This can be part of a kickoff or a regular feature of your classes.

- Explain the role of the pastor in modeling prayer and cast a vision for establishing prayer DNA in the church.

- Introduce the new members to leaders who facilitate the prayer ministry.

- Describe various prayer initiatives the church has taken or has planned. Introduce opportunities for the new members to get involved.

- Teach the group a simple prayer strategy (such as the ACTS paradigm).

- Enlist a commitment from longer-term members to pray for the new members regularly for at least three months.

- Spend additional time together in prayer as the class concludes. Make it almost impossible for a new member to complete the class without knowing how much prayer matters to your church.

Emphasize the importance of prayer as you seek workers for your church.

Jesus made it clear that faithful laborers are to pray for more laborers (Luke 10:1-2). This means that those of us who serve must continually pray and watch for the new workers that God is raising up. We pray as we go, not waiting for an opening in the church workforce before we start to pray. We pray and trust that God is already preparing the next generation of workers for our church. This role of ongoing prayer for additional workers for the harvest might be part of the responsibility taken on by a prayer team.

Ask about the prayer life of potential workers as you enlist them to serve. In my forty-plus years of ministry in different settings, I don't recall any interview that included a question about my prayer life. Perhaps those who were recruiting me assumed my commitment to prayer. But, truth be told, no one we recruit to serve in God's church warrants that assumption. If prayer is as important as we believe, it is worth asking any potential church worker about his or her prayer life. At a minimum, you should want workers who are committed to growing in prayer even if they have a lot of room for growth. That is part of the discipleship process (Luke 11:1-13).

Pray for workers for the harvest, and make sure they pray. With prayerful recruiting, your church shouldn't have to jump-start the prayer life of those already in places of service. A commitment to prayer should naturally become part of the church's DNA.

Establish prayer coordinators in every small group and individual ministry.

When I teach my discipleship class, I argue that discipleship occurs at three levels: the corporate level, where worship itself trains believers to follow God; the small group level, where discipleship is more connected to life-on-life training and fellowship; and the mentoring level, where one believer invests deeply in one to three other believers. In my judgment, the small group level offers the best opportunity for increasing prayer in the church. It offers more opportunities to train believers individually than the corporate-level worship service does, and it typically involves more members than mentoring does.

To utilize small groups to expand prayer in the church, however, requires *intention* and *strategy*. Thus, the role of a prayer coordinator, whose life should already exhibit a strong commitment to prayer, is multifold:

- Keep prayer central in all activities of the small group. The goal is that group members will come to assume that prayer will be part of each gathering.

- Seek prayer requests from the group, and share them with the entire group (with permission, of course). As God answers prayers, the prayer coordinator is responsible for informing the group so they can praise God together.

- Serve as a liaison with the church's overall prayer team, helping to promote churchwide prayer efforts.

Leaders of individual church ministries or teams can follow that same pattern. The leaders themselves may take responsibility for leading their members to pray—as John and Faye did in my church—or they may enlist someone else in their group to help prioritize prayer in their ministry or team. The formula is simple: If your church has more laypeople committed to leading prayer in their respective small groups and ministries, your church will be more of a praying church. Enlist leaders accordingly.

Use your small groups strategically to cover the church in prayer.

Small groups offer not only fellowship and equipping, but also ways for the group to pray for the entire church. The group prayer coordinator can lead the efforts, but the groups need to be given a plan. Consider, for example, this yearly plan for small groups to pray:

- *January:* Pray for the church's leaders.

- *February:* Pray for another adult small group in the church.

- *March:* Pray for the church's outreach efforts during the upcoming Easter season.

- *April:* Pray for a next generation group (children's or student classes).

- *May:* Pray for the church's efforts to reach the community.

- *June:* Pray for all the small group and ministry leaders.

- *July:* Pray for another ministry team in the church.

- *August:* Pray for community and local school leaders.

- *September:* Pray for the worship service each week during the month.

- *October:* Pray for laborers to continue the work of ministry, including the "called out" ones who might take the gospel to the ends of the earth.

- *November:* Pray prayers of thanksgiving for what the Lord has done through your church.

- *December:* Pray for the church's outreach during the Christmas season.

Your church may not adopt every one of these emphases, but choose some that will focus the prayers of your small groups. Make sure the small group leaders and the prayer coordinator are ready and willing to cast vision for the task, and lead the group to pray together each week for the respective needs. Your groups will become more prayer-centered and others-focused as a result.

Turn your church's list of activities into a churchwide prayer list.

I have previously mentioned Brother Jack, my pastoral hero. He kept the church bulletin from every Sunday he preached for more than fifty years. The bulletins were snapshots of what the church was doing at a given time, and Brother Jack could relive ministry memories each time he looked at an old bulletin.

Many churches no longer use a bulletin, but most churches have some means of informing the congregation about current and upcoming events. Our church uses bulletins and an electronic calendar on our website to keep the church informed. Most of the time, I suspect, church members quickly review the bulletin on Sunday morning only to see if any activities pertain to them. Others turn to the website to check details and perhaps to register for activities they have decided to attend. Few, if any, view the bulletin or calendar as a prayer list.

But if you think about it, your church's activity ledger is a ready-made prayer list. If the student group is meeting for a Bible study on Monday night, I want to pray for them. If the mom's group is meeting on Thursday morning, I should pray for them, too. If an outreach event is scheduled for Saturday morning, surely I should want to intercede for the participants. There's no need to invent a new prayer list; just use the one already created.

Individuals and families can pray this way each day. Small groups might pray briefly about the events when they meet weekly. You might even use this list on Sunday morning to guide the congregation in silently praying for all the church has planned for the upcoming week. Only God knows how our scheduled activities might be stronger and more fruitful if our congregations intentionally prayed about them. In fact, participation in events might even increase when members are praying about each event.

At least annually, schedule a one- or two-day training
to renew your church's passion for prayer.

Even the best prayer warriors need to stoke the fire again at times. I love to pray, but I still find myself inspired and challenged when I learn from others who are much more committed to prayer than I am. Most of our church members are busy, but that shouldn't keep us from scheduling important trainings in prayer.

What is the secret to making this strategy work? One approach is to get the best speaker you can. Pray first and see who God brings to mind. Look for someone who speaks from experience with clarity and passion. Seek recommendations from other trusted leaders. Listen to presentations online if someone recommends a speaker you don't know. A poor speaker will not only defeat the purpose of the current training, but he or she may also hinder recruiting for future events. Given the difficulty of growing prayer warriors in general, it's tough to overcome a bad prayer training session.

Next, personally recruit members to attend. Generic announcements from the pulpit or in the bulletin will likely not lead to increased attendance. Recruit face-to-face, eyeball-to-eyeball, believer-to-believer. Start with your small group and ministry leaders, and ask them to help you recruit. Let your passion for the event inspire others to attend.

The point is this: Do *something* with prayer and persevere in your efforts. Soon the prayer DNA in your congregation will increase.

Overcome Your Inertia

I call myself a "focused procrastinator." I tend to put things off until they absolutely must get done, but then I get after it with some real vigor. Every time I am stressed out by a deadline, I try to convince myself to change my habits; but nothing has changed yet. I still function best when the pressure is on.

Fortunately, when I finally get started on a task, I become extremely focused. Get me on a roll, and I will work with diligence until the assignment is finished. I don't claim this approach is the best one—I sometimes find it hard to sleep because my mind is so focused—but intensity for the task marks everything I do.

Here is my challenge to you as you strive to develop DNA-level prayer in your church. Learn from my mistakes—that is, do not delay getting started—and focus on the task at hand. Like a laser beam, turn your attention to leading your church to its knees. There, you and your congregation will find the power of God waiting for you.

One Caution and
a Final Challenge

THIS ENTIRE BOOK is about unleashing the potential and power of a praying church. Before we conclude, however, I want to offer one caution and a final challenge.

First, the caution. I have occasionally met prayer warriors who pray a lot but do little else. They are motivated to go to the mountaintop to meet with the Father, but they may not want to come back down to deal with a nonbelieving world. Their prayer closet becomes a retreat from the world rather than a place to get reinvigorated for effective great commission living.

Prayer is powerful, but prayer by itself is insufficient. God calls us to pray—yes. But he has also commissioned us to go and make disciples. Consider the following examples of times when we need to do more than pray:

1. **When we are praying for someone to get saved, but we haven't made any attempt to share the gospel with him or her.** God is certainly sovereign over salvation, but he uses us to tell the story.

2. **When we are praying for God to bring a wayward believer back into the fold, but we are unwilling to lovingly confront that believer.** Again, God calls us to help restore fallen brothers and sisters (Galatians 6:1).

3. **When we pray for God to provide financially for our church, but we have offered no stewardship training for our members.** Why should God provide when we have not done the work of discipleship?

4. **When we are asking God to free us from a controlling sin, but we keep putting ourselves in the same wrong place . . . with the same wrong people . . . at the same wrong time.** Praying for freedom without also choosing wisely is toying with God.

5. **When we are pleading with God to give us clarity about an issue, but we have not opened his Word on a regular basis in a long time.** We should not expect God to answer our request when we ignore his primary means of speaking to us.

6. **When we are asking God to show us his will, but we already know what we are going to do, regardless.** Prayer is superfluous when we have already decided we're going to follow our own will over God's.

7. **When we are pleading with God to give us mature believers to help lead the congregation, but we have no equipping strategy in place to raise them up.** Churches with no intentional discipleship strategy seldom develop a good leadership pipeline.

8. **When we are praying about our needs, but are not repenting from our wrongs.** Unconfessed sin in unrepentant hearts clogs the prayer channel (Isaiah 59:1-2).

9. **When we are praying about something, but not forgiving someone who has wounded us.** Here is how Jesus addressed this issue: "I tell you, you can pray for anything, and if you believe that you've received it, it will be yours. But when you are praying, first forgive anyone you are holding a grudge against, so that your Father in heaven will forgive your sins, too" (Mark 11:24-25).

10. **When we are praying for God to use us as we preach or teach, but we have been lazy in our preparation during the week.** Thank God his Word is powerful beyond our feeble efforts, but we cannot assume that God will bless our poor work ethic.[1]

Next, the concluding challenge. A. W. Tozer, the well-known twentieth-century pastor and author, reminded his readers about the incredible power of prayer with these words:

What profit is there in prayer? "Much every way." Whatever God can do faith can do, and whatever faith can do prayer can do when it is offered in faith. An invitation to prayer is, therefore, an invitation to omnipotence, for prayer engages the omnipotent God and brings Him into our human affairs.[2]

Tozer's words ought to give us great pause and produce in us great humility. Through prayer, we tap into the power of the omnipotent God.

It is what Tozer says next that arrests me and challenges me as I finish this book:

> Nothing is impossible to the [person] who prays in faith, just as nothing is impossible with God. This generation has yet to prove all that prayer can do for believing men and women.[3]

I encourage you to read that last line again: "This generation has yet to prove all that prayer can do for believing men and women." That is a gripping statement that challenges me as a church leader. Tozer believed his generation had not yet experienced the full power of prayer, and I'm sure he would say the same about our generation. If we have not yet experienced "all that prayer can do," we must long for something different, something more. We must long for prayer to become part of the DNA in our churches.

Pursuing that goal starts right here. With me. With you. With my church and your church. There is, after all, untold power in a church that prays together.

> *Almighty Father, teach us to pray. May we long to spend time with you and enjoy communicating with you. Empower us to raise up other prayer warriors who help us reach our neighbors and the nations with the gospel. Thank you for your faithfulness in continually calling us to prayer.*

Notes

CHAPTER 1: WHY NO POWER?

1. Tracy Munsil, "AWVI 2020 Survey: 1 in 3 US Adults Embrace Salvation through Jesus; More Believe It Can Be 'Earned,'" Cultural Research Center at Arizona Christian University, August 4, 2020, https://www.arizonachristian.edu/2020/08/04/1-in-3-us-adults-embrace-salvation-through-jesus-more-believe-it-can-be-earned/.
2. Munsil, "AWVI 2020 Survey."
3. Donald A. McGavran, *Understanding Church Growth*, ed. C. Peter Wagner, 3rd ed. (Grand Rapids, MI: Eerdmans, 1990), 19.
4. McGavran, *Understanding Church Growth*.
5. McGavran, *Understanding Church Growth*.
6. Adapted from Chuck Lawless, "Churches That Only Talk about Prayer or Churches That Really Pray?," (blog), March 29, 2017, http://chucklawless.com/2017/03/churches-that-only-talk-about-prayer-or-churches-that-really-pray/; and Chuck Lawless, *Discipled Warriors* (Grand Rapids, MI: Kregel, 2002), 158.
7. Chuck Lawless, *Lord, Teach Us Pastors to Pray!* (Franklin, TN: Church Answers, 2021), 14–17. See also William F. Cook III and Chuck Lawless, *Spiritual Warfare in the Storyline of Scripture* (Nashville: B&H Academic, 2019), 279, 306–307.
8. Cook and Lawless, *Spiritual Warfare in the Storyline of Scripture*, 315.
9. Cook and Lawless, *Spiritual Warfare in the Storyline of Scripture*, 244.
10. Jack R. Taylor, *Prayer: Life's Limitless Reach* (Nashville: Broadman Press, 1977), 35.
11. John Onwuchekwa, *Prayer: How Praying Together Shapes the Church* (Wheaton, IL: Crossway, 2018), 39.
12. Megan Briggs, "Do You Read Your Bible Everyday? Most Churchgoers

Say No," *ChurchLeaders* (blog), July 25, 2019, https://churchleaders
.com/news/356089-do-you-read-your-bible-everyday-most-churchgoers
-say-no.html.

13. Charles Haddon Spurgeon, *The Soul Winner* (Grand Rapids, MI:
    Eerdmans, 1963), 17.

14. For example, see Tom Elliff, *A Passion for Prayer: Experiencing Deeper
    Intimacy with God* (Fort Washington, PA: CLC Publications, 2010).

15. See similar descriptions in Charles E. Lawless Jr., *Serving in Your Church
    Prayer Ministry* (Grand Rapids, MI: Zondervan, 2003), 17; and Lawless,
    Lord, Teach Us Pastors to Pray!, 27.

CHAPTER 2: WHAT PRAYER IS, AND WHY IT MATTERS

1. Lisa Tawn Bergren, *God Gave Us Prayer* (Colorado Springs: Waterbrook,
   2021), np.

2. J. Gary Millar, *Calling on the Name of the Lord: A Biblical Theology of
   Prayer* (Downers Grove, IL: InterVarsity Press, 2016), 27.

3. Timothy Keller, *Prayer: Experiencing Awe and Intimacy with God* (New
   York: Penguin, 2014), 45. Italics in the original.

4. R. C. Sproul, *Does Prayer Change Things?* (Sanford, FL: Reformation Trust,
   2009), 11.

5. Stephen Kendrick and Alex Kendrick, *The Battle Plan for Prayer* (Nashville:
   B&H Publishing, 2015), 36–37.

6. Gregg R. Allison, *The Baker Compact Dictionary of Theological Terms*
   (Grand Rapids, MI: Baker, 2016), 165.

7. Chuck Lawless, *Lord, Teach Us Pastors to Pray* (Franklin, TN: Church
   Answers, 2021), 5.

8. J. I. Packer and Carolyn Nystrom, *Praying: Finding Our Way through Duty
   to Delight* (Downers Grove, IL: IVP, 2006), 21–31.

9. Kendrick and Kendrick, *Battle Plan*, 33–34.

10. Ben Patterson, *God's Prayer Book: The Power and Pleasure of Praying the
    Psalms* (Carol Stream, IL: SaltRiver, 2008), 2.

11. Andrew Murray, *With Christ in the School of Prayer* (The New Christian
    Classics Library, 2018), 143.

12. J. I. Packer and Carolyn Nystrom include a similar—though not exact—
    list on page 148 of *Praying*.

13. Packer and Nystrom, *Praying*, 148. Italics in the original.

14. D. A. Carson, *Praying with Paul: A Call to Spiritual Reformation* (Grand
    Rapids, MI: Baker Academic, 2015), ix.

15. Cheryl Sacks, *The Prayer-Saturated Church: A Comprehensive Handbook
    for Prayer Leaders* (Colorado Springs: NavPress, 2007), 23–24.

16. Packer and Nystrom, *Praying*, 216. Italics added.

17. Gregory R. Frizzell, *How to Develop a Powerful Prayer Life* (Memphis: Master Design, 1999), 32.

18. Frizzell, *How to Develop a Powerful Prayer Life*, 33-35.

CHAPTER 3: PRAYING LIKE JESUS AND THE EARLY CHURCH

1. Andrew Murray, *With Christ in the School of Prayer* (The New Christian Classics Library, 2018), 9.

2. Adapted from Chuck Lawless, *Lord, Teach Us Pastors to Pray!* (Franklin, TN: Church Answers, 2021), 6–7.

3. Thom S. Rainer, "Dispelling the 80 Percent Myth of Declining Churches," Church Answers (blog), June 28, 2017, https://churchanswers.com/blog /dispelling-80-percent-myth-declining-churches/; and Aubrey Malphurs, "The State of the American Church: Plateaued or Declining," The Malphurs Group (blog), September 5, 2014, https://malphursgroup .com/state-of-the-american-church-plateaued-declining/.

4. John B. Polhill, *Acts*, New American Commentary (Nashville: Broadman & Holman, 1992), 90.

5. Grant R. Osborne, ed., *Acts*, Life Application Bible Commentary (Carol Stream, IL: Tyndale House, 1999), 15.

6. Gary Millar, *Calling on the Name of the Lord: A Biblical Theology of Prayer* (Downers Grove, IL: IVP Academic, 2016), 197.

7. Adapted from Lawless, *Lord, Teach Us Pastors to Pray!*, 35–36.

8. John Onwuchekwa, *Prayer: How Praying Together Shapes the Church* (Wheaton, IL: Crossway, 2018), 18.

CHAPTER 4: THE BATTLE OF PRAYER

1. Clinton E. Arnold, *3 Crucial Questions about Spiritual Warfare* (Grand Rapids, MI: Baker, 1997), 43.

2. Adapted from Chuck Lawless, "11 Reasons Church Leaders Struggle with Prayer," (blog), August 1, 2021, http://chucklawless.com/2018/01 /11-reasons-church-leaders-struggle-with-prayer/; Chuck Lawless, *Lord, Teach Us Pastors to Pray!* (Franklin, TN: Church Answers, 2021), 8–10.

3. Steven R. Miller, *Daniel*, New American Commentary (Nashville: Broadman & Holman, 1994), 182.

4. Hal M. Haller Jr., *The Gospel according to Matthew*, Grace New Testament Commentary (Denton, TX: Grace Evangelical Society, 2010), 31.

5. D. A. Carson, *The Gospel according to John*, Pillar New Testament Commentary (Grand Rapids, MI: Eerdmans, 1991), 565.

6. John Franklin and Chuck Lawless, *Spiritual Warfare: Biblical Truth for Victory* (Nashville: Lifeway, 2001).

7. Arnold, *3 Crucial Questions*, 42–43.

8. See also William F. Cook III and Chuck Lawless, *Spiritual Warfare in the Storyline of Scripture* (Nashville: B&H Academic, 2019), 251–252, 279.

CHAPTER 5: PRAYING LEADERS

1. D. A. Carson, *Praying with Paul: A Call to Spiritual Reformation* (Grand Rapids, MI: Baker, 2015), 16.
2. J. Oswald Sanders, *Spiritual Leadership: Principles of Excellence for Every Believer* (Chicago: Moody, 2007), 83, 90, 91.
3. See Chuck Lawless, "The Prayer of Joshua," in *Praying at the Crossroads*, ed. Ken Coley (Nashville: Lifeway, 2019), 30–45.
4. Gerald F. Hawthorne, Ralph P. Martin, and Daniel G. Reid, eds., *Dictionary of Paul and His Letters* (Downers Grove, IL: IVP Academic, 2009), 725.
5. E. M. Bounds, *Pastor and Prayer: Why and How Pastors Ought to Pray* (Abbotsford, WI: Aneko Press, 2018), 112.
6. See also Chuck Lawless, "5 Reasons Many Pastors Struggle with Prayer—and What to Do about It," (blog), May 2, 2019, http://chucklawless .com/2019/05/5-reasons-many-pastors-struggle-with-prayer-and-what-to -do-about-it/.
7. Jim Cymbala, *Fresh Wind, Fresh Fire: What Happens When God's Spirit Invades the Hearts of His People* (Grand Rapids, MI: Zondervan, 1997), 56.
8. C. Peter Wagner, *Churches That Pray: How Prayer Can Help Revitalize Your Church and Break Down the Walls between You and Your Community* (Ventura, CA: Regal, 1993), 84–85.
9. Tom Elliff, *A Passion for Prayer: Experiencing Deeper Intimacy with God* (Port Washington, PA: CLC Publications, 2010).
10. Elliff, *A Passion for Prayer*, 19–20. Italics in the original.
11. Adapted from Chuck Lawless, "8 Ways I Pray for My Wife," (blog), June 16, 2020, http://chucklawless.com/2020/06/8-ways-i-pray-for-my-wife/; Lawless, *Lord, Teach Us Pastors to Pray!* (Franklin, TN: Church Answers, 2021), 25.
12. Ronnie Floyd, "Worship Services Need to Recover Pastor-Led Prayer," *Christian Post*, June 25, 2017, https://www.christianpost.com/news /worship-services-need-recover-pastor-led-prayer.html; and Ronnie Floyd, *How to Pray* (Nashville: Thomas Nelson, 2019).
13. Lawless, *Lord, Teach Us Pastors to Pray!*, 12.

CHAPTER 6: GETTING STARTED: PRAYING TOGETHER

1. "Charles H. Spurgeon: Did You Know?" Christian History Institute, accessed September 27, 2021, https://christianhistoryinstitute .org/magazine/article/spurgeon-did-you-know.

2. Charles Spurgeon, "Prayer Meetings," The Charles Spurgeon Sermon Collection, sermon #3421, https://www.thekingdomcollective .com/spurgeon/sermon/3421/.

3. Kenneth A. Mathews, *Genesis 1–11:26,* New American Commentary (Nashville: Broadman & Holman, 1996), 213.

4. See also John Onwuchekwa, *Prayer: How Praying Together Shapes the Church* (Wheaton, IL: Crossway, 2018), 41; and R. Albert Mohler, *The Prayer That Turns the World Upside Down* (Nashville: Thomas Nelson, 2018), 42–46.

5. Clinton E. Arnold, *3 Crucial Questions about Spiritual Warfare* (Grand Rapids, MI: Baker, 1997), 45.

6. Robert D. Dale, *To Dream Again: How to Help Your Church Come Alive* (Nashville: Broadman Press, 1981), 15.

7. Dale, *To Dream Again,* 16.

8. Dale, *To Dream Again,* 17.

9. John Onwuchekwa, *Prayer: How Praying Together Shapes the Church* (Wheaton, IL: Crossway, 2018), 99–100.

10. Onwuchekwa, *Prayer,* 99, 100.

11. Onwuchekwa, *Prayer,* 104.

12. Chuck Lawless, *Membership Matters: Insights from Effective Churches on New Member Classes and Assimilation* (Grand Rapids, MI: Zondervan, 2005), 65.

CHAPTER 7: ONE CAUTION AND A FINAL CHALLENGE

1. Adapted from Chuck Lawless, "10 Times When Prayer Is Not Enough," (blog), July 27, 2021, http://chucklawless.com/2021/07/10-times-when -prayer-is-not-enough/.

2. A. W. Tozer, *Prayer: Communing with God in Everything—Collected Insights from A. W. Tozer* (Chicago: Moody, 2016), 88.

3. Tozer, *Prayer,* 88.

About the Author

Chuck Lawless CURRENTLY SERVES as professor of evangelism and missions, dean of doctoral studies, and vice president for spiritual formation and ministry centers at Southeastern Seminary. He has served as a pastor for almost twenty years and is the author or editor of ten books, including *Spiritual Warfare, Discipled Warriors, Making Disciples through Mentoring, Serving in Your Church's Prayer Ministry,* and *Spiritual Warfare in the Storyline of Scripture.* Dr. Lawless speaks extensively around the country and lives with his wife, Pam, in Wake Forest, North Carolina.

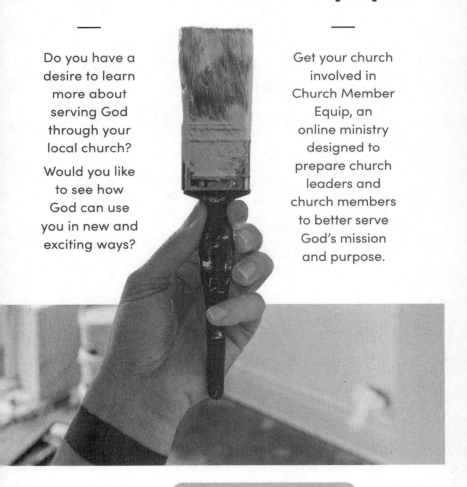